Virtual exchange: towards digital equity in internationalisation

Edited by Müge Satar

Published by Research-publishing.net, a not-for-profit association
Contact: info@research-publishing.net

© 2021 by Editor (collective work)
© 2021 by Authors (individual work)

Virtual exchange: towards digital equity in internationalisation
Edited by Müge Satar

Publication date: 2021/08/16

Rights: the whole volume is published under the Attribution-NonCommercial-NoDerivatives International (CC BY-NC-ND) licence. Under the CC BY-NC-ND licence, the volume is freely available online (https://doi.org/10.14705/rpnet.2021.53.9782490057955) for anybody to read, download, copy, and redistribute provided that the author(s), editorial team, and publisher are properly cited. Commercial use and derivative works are, however, not permitted.

Disclaimer: Research-publishing.net does not take any responsibility for the content of the pages written by the authors of this book. The authors have recognised that the work described was not published before, or that it was not under consideration for publication elsewhere. While the information in this book is believed to be true and accurate on the date of its going to press, neither the editorial team nor the publisher can accept any legal responsibility for any errors or omissions. The publisher makes no warranty, expressed or implied, with respect to the material contained herein. While Research-publishing.net is committed to publishing works of integrity, the words are the authors' alone.

Trademark notice: product or corporate names may be trademarks or registered trademarks, and are used only for identification and explanation without intent to infringe.

Copyrighted material: every effort has been made by the editorial team to trace copyright holders and to obtain their permission for the use of copyrighted material in this book. In the event of errors or omissions, please notify the publisher of any corrections that will need to be incorporated in future editions of this book.

Typeset by Research-publishing.net
Cover illustration by © ryzhi - stock.adobe.com
Cover layout by © 2021 Raphaël Savina (raphael@savina.net)

ISBN13: 978-2-490057-95-5 (Ebook, PDF, colour)
ISBN13: 978-2-490057-96-2 (Ebook, EPUB, colour)
ISBN13: 978-2-490057-94-8 (Paperback - Print on demand, black and white)
Print on demand technology is a high-quality, innovative and ecological printing method; with which the book is never 'out of stock' or 'out of print'.

British Library Cataloguing-in-Publication Data.
A cataloguing record for this book is available from the British Library.

Legal deposit, France: Bibliothèque Nationale de France - Dépôt légal: août 2021.

Table of contents

v   Notes on contributors

1   Introducing virtual exchange: towards digital equity in internationalisation
Müge Satar

Section 1. The local and the global

17   Intercultural youth: the global generation and virtual exchange
Patricia Szobonya and Catherine Roche

29   Can COIL be effective in using diversity to contribute to equality? Experiences of iKudu, a European-South African consortium operating via a decolonised approach to project delivery
Alun DeWinter and Reinout Klamer

41   The multi-disciplinary approach to an interdisciplinary virtual exchange
Paula Fonseca, Kristi Julian, Wendi Hulme, Maria De Lurdes Martins, and Regina Brautlacht

51   Creating a prototype for a seawater farm through an American-Tunisian virtual exchange
Nadia Cheikhrouhou and Kenneth Ludwig

Section 2. Digital communication skills

63   Compensatory strategies adopted by Chinese EFL learners in virtual exchange with native speakers
Ruiling Feng and Sheida Shirvani

73   Supporting intercultural communication with visual information in virtual exchanges: when a picture paints a thousand words
Marta Fondo

Section 3. Multisensory VE projects

85   Making the virtual tangible: using visual thinking to enhance online transnational learning
Kelly M. Murdoch-Kitt and Denielle J. Emans

101   Virtual exchange facilitated by interactive, digital, cultural artefacts: communities, languages, and activities app (ENACT)
Colin B. Dodds, Alison Whelan, Ahmed Kharrufa, and Müge Satar

113   Building empathy through a comparative study of popular cultures in Caracas, Venezuela, and Albany, United States
José Luis Jiménez and Ilka Kressner

Section 4. Staff and student voices

131   Educational innovation in times of crisis: learner voices from the Albany-Caracas COIL exchange
Sofía Ruiz, Santiago Hernández, Alicia García, and Jesús Chacón

139   Virtual exchange: from students' expectations to perceived outcomes
Elke Nissen, Catherine Felce, and Catherine Muller

157   Continuous professional development on virtual exchange in Europe: insights from the Erasmus+ VE introductory online course
Ana Beaven and Gillian Davies

169   Author index

Notes on contributors

Editor

Dr Müge Satar is Lecturer in applied linguistics and TESOL at Newcastle University, UK. She is Primary Investigator of the ENACT project (https://enacteuropa.com/). She is interested in communicative and pedagogical aspects of multimodal interaction for online language learning and teaching, focusing on social presence, meaning-making, instruction-giving, and translanguaging.

Authors

Dr Ana Beaven teaches English as a foreign language at the University of Bologna Language Centre. She has a PhD in applied linguistics, and has taken part in many European projects. Her main areas of interest are virtual exchange, intercultural language learning and teaching, and the use of technology to enhance pedagogical practices.

Regina Brautlacht is Senior Lecturer in English and business communication at Bonn-Rhein-Sieg University of Applied Sciences, Germany. She has been appointed as Presidential Advisor for Global Digital Learning since 2018. She coordinates the English program for the Department of Management Sciences and was awarded the university teaching award for her innovative blended-learning course 'Business English, a Simulation Course in Entrepreneurship'. She holds a Master's degree in educational media from the University of Duisburg-Essen and a double major in German and International Relations from George Mason University, USA.

Jesús Chacón is a senior communication student with audiovisual production and marketing concentrations, from the Andrés Bello Catholic University, with experience working as a graphic designer and a sales and advertising advisor. He is a participant in the COIL interuniversity (2019-2020) between the State University of New York and UCAB, and co-creator of the documentary *Educational Innovation in Times of Crisis*.

v

Notes on contributors

Nadia Cheikhrouhou is a lecturer of entrepreneurship and innovation at the High Institute of Technological Studies of Béja (HITSB). She graduated from the Institute of Commercial Higher Studies of Carthage and has a Master degree in marketing. She is a trainer at L'Essor Technologique de Béja Incubator. She coaches students at hackathons, innovation challenges, and ideation camps. She facilitates design thinking workshops at the Career Center of HITSB.

Gillian Davies is an English language teacher at the Language Centre, University of Padova, Italy. She has a PGCE in teaching English for academic purposes from the University of Nottingham. Her interests include learner autonomy, virtual exchange, and technology in language learning and teaching.

Dr Alun DeWinter is Research Fellow for Coventry University's Centre for Global Learning. His research interests include the internationalisation of higher education, internationalisation at home, collaborative online international learning, global citizenship, and decolonisation of the curriculum. Alun is currently involved with both Workgroups 1 and 2 of the iKudu project.

Colin B. Dodds is a research software engineer and PhD candidate at Open Lab, Newcastle University, UK. He loves bringing user-centred software designs to life and has a special interest in music-related software development and research.

Associate Professor **Dr Denielle Emans** specializes in the area of communication design, with an emphasis on bringing together intercultural perspectives and participatory practices to fuel creative action. She completed her PhD at the University of Queensland's Centre for Communication and Social Change. She has taught in the MENA region since 2011.

Dr Catherine Felce is a senior lecturer at University of Grenoble Alpes (France). She teaches German as a foreign language, and her research focuses on syntactic and discursive acquisitions through usage and interactions. More recently, she has also been interested in CALL, and the impact of virtual exchange on the development of language skills.

Notes on contributors

Ruiling Feng is an assistant professor and virtual exchange coordinator at the Foreign Languages College, Tianjin Normal University, and doctoral student of applied linguistics at Tsinghua University. She has practiced virtual exchange for five years. Her research interests lie in second language acquisition, corpus linguistics, and academic English writing.

Marta Fondo is an expert in innovation in education. She works in multidisciplinary environments as a project designer, coordinator, researcher, and teacher. She's highly interested in technology enhanced learning, especially in intercultural and affective factors. Marta is about to submit her PhD in education and ICT at Universitat Oberta de Catalunya.

Dr Paula Fonseca is Adjunct Professor at the Polytechnic Institute of Viseu (Portugal) and visiting Professor at the Universidade Católica Portuguesa (Portugal). She holds a PhD degree (2016) in advanced English studies. She has been teaching English and Spanish as a foreign language in higher education for 25 years. She has collaborated in a number of international projects and has also participated in international conferences. Her research interests include: virtual exchange, technology in foreign language teaching/learning, cognitive linguistics, multimodality, and political humour.

Alicia García is a communication student from the Andrés Bello Catholic University, audiovisual production and marketing concentrations. She is a TV producer in the international channel IVC, with the 'Mundo de Mujeres' program, a participant in the COIL Project (2019-2020) between the State University of New York and UCAB, and a co-creator of the documentary *Educational Innovation in Times of Crisis*.

Santiago Hernández is an actor and communication graduate from the Andrés Bello Catholic University, audiovisual production and journalism concentrations, and a yoga alliance RYT 200 certified instructor. He is an English tutor, a participant in the COIL Project (2019-2020) between the State University of New York and UCAB, and co-creator and co-director of the documentary *Educational Innovation in Times of Crisis*.

Notes on contributors

Wendi Hulme is Professor in the School of Engineering and Technology at Conestoga College ITAL, teaching in the Bachelor of Interior Design (Honours) Program since 2012 where she also served as Program Coordinator for four years. As a registered (educator) interior designer with ARIDO, Wendi has 20+ years of practical experience in Canada and the USA on residential and commercial projects including retail, hospitality, and corporate design. She is Council for Interior Design Accreditation Site Visitor and LEED Accredited Professional, with her research interests focused on sustainability and virtual exchange.

José Luis Jiménez is COIL Coordinator at Catholic University Andrés Bello. His research areas include virtual exchange, transmedia journalism, democracy, and human rights. He is a PhD candidate in comparative studies at Florida Atlantic University. In 1991, he worked as journalist for the World Conservation Union (IUCN); in 1993 he was honored with a full scholarship from the Organization of American States to pursue his Master's degree in arts at the American University. In 1999 he worked at the University of Florida as Coordinator for the Welfare to Work program and presented "Moving Wages Clients to Sustainable Employment in the Food Service Industry" at the CYFAR 2000 National Conference, Charlotte, N.C.

Dr Kristi Julian is Professor and Program Coordinator in interior design at Middle Tennessee State University. Prof Dr Julian is a registered interior designer with experience in facilities design, healthcare, hospitality, and construction. Dr Julian is Council for Interior Design Accreditation Site Visitor Chair and has over 30 years of practical experience in the field. Her research interests focus on interior design pedagogy and sustainability. She is a scholarship reviewer for numerous journals including ASEE, JET, and IDEC. Dr Julian is an accredited professional with LEED (BD+C), EDAC, and WELL.

Dr Ahmed Kharrufa is a senior lecturer in human-computer interaction at Open Lab, Newcastle University, UK. He leads the educational technology research at Open Lab and his research in this area focuses on the design, development, implementation, and evaluation of processes and technologies in support of learning, school-community engagement, and cultural and language learning.

Notes on contributors

Reinout Klamer is from The Hague University of Applied Sciences. He views Collaborative Online International Learning (COIL) from three different perspectives. As a lecturer and coordinator of COIL projects, he is a researcher participating in the research group Global Learning studying COIL and its relations to internationalisation at home, and as a coach, he coaches others in setting up and running COIL projects. Reinout is involved in both Workgroups 1 and 2 of the iKudu project.

Dr Ilka Kressner is Associate Professor of Spanish at UAlbany, SUNY. Her scholarship and teaching examine Spanish American literature and film and visual arts (20th-21st centuries) from a variety of cultural and national contexts. She is interested in theoretical approaches to conceptions of space in art, intermediality, ecocriticism, as well as collaborative teaching methods.

Kenneth Ludwig is Lecturer at University of Michigan since 2001. He created courses in entrepreneurship and innovation including: Engineering for Community, The Art of Entrepreneurship, The Innovator's Toolkit, and Creating Innovative Environments. Mentor and advisor to optiMIze and individual students, invited speaker to Undergraduate Research Opportunities, Society of Women Engineers, and other student groups, he is also a startup founder in publishing, computer simulations for education, revenue based finance, and others, with small company consulting. Experience in community based, community college and university teaching, angel finance, venture capital funding, community organizing, and child advocacy, he holds a BS in sociology, and an MLS in technology education from Eastern Michigan University.

Dr Maria De Lurdes Martins is Adjunct Professor at the Polytechnic Institute of Viseu, Portugal, where she teaches English for tourism to undergraduate students. She holds a PhD in linguistics (2012). Her research interests include dialogical and dialectical language learning, and telecollaboration projects across cultures. She has been part of virtual exchange projects since 2014. The participation in these projects has allowed the participation in international conferences and some publications. She has Postgraduate Education in Multimedia in Education Between 2012 and 2018, she coordinated Erasmus +

Notes on contributors

mobility in her department and was co-responsible for the creation of three international semesters.

Dr Catherine Muller is a senior lecturer at University Grenoble Alpes (France) where she teaches foreign language education in the Masters programme teaching French as a foreign language. Inside the Lidilem research team, she explores intercultural dimensions and teacher cognition, among others in CALL settings.

Assistant Professor **Kelly M. Murdoch-Kitt** is a designer focused on interpersonal interactions and social responsibility. She co-authored the book Intercultural Collaboration by Design with Dr Denielle Emans, which introduces over 30 of their visual thinking activities to support COIL. She recently beta-launched a collaboration-matching platform for faculty, orbit-teams.com.

Dr Elke Nissen is Full Professor at University Grenoble Alpes (France). Her research and teaching focus on blended and online learning, specifically course design, online communication, virtual exchange, and tuition within CALL. She coordinates research within the Erasmus+ EVOLVE project.

Catherine Roche is a professor in the Business Department at SUNY Rockland Community College in Suffern, New York. In 2013 she received the SUNY Chancellor's Award for Excellence in Teaching. She has co-authored three articles published in the Journal of Educational Technology. She serves as the campus COIL Coordinator.

Sofía Ruiz is a communication student from the Andrés Bello Catholic University, audiovisual production and marketing concentrations. She is a participant in the COIL interuniversity (2019-2020) project between the State University of New York (SUNY) and UCAB, and co-creator and co-editor of the documentary of the SUNY-UCAB experience entitled: *Educational Innovation in Times of Crisis*.

Dr Müge Satar, see Editor's section.

Dr Sheida Shirvani is Full Professor, Emeriti of Communication Studies. She has been a COIL Fellow since 2015 and was a member of the COIL advisory committee during 2016-2019. She is a professional interpreter in the health environment. She has taught communication studies courses for 33 years.

Patricia Szobonya is Associate Professor and Program Director of the legal studies, paralegal studies, criminal justice, and corporate homeland security programs at Rockland Community College. She is a graduate of New York Law School and licensed to practice law in New York and New Jersey.

Dr Alison Whelan is Research Associate in the School of Education, Communication, and Language Sciences at Newcastle University. She has a particular interest in language teaching and learning, and enjoys collaborating with teachers and students to develop, support, and embed curriculum innovations.

Reviewers

- Anna Beaven, *University of Bologna, Italy*
- Regina Brautlacht, *Bonn-Rhein-Sieg University of Applied Sciences, Germany*
- Nadia Cheikhrouhou, *High Institute of Technological Studies of Béja, Tunisia*
- Izzy Crawford, *Robert Gordon University, Scotland*
- Gillian Davies, *University of Padua, Italy*
- Alun DeWinter, *Coventry University, United Kingdom*
- Denielle J. Emans, *Roger Williams University, United States*
- Catherine Felce, *Université Grenoble Alpes / LIDILEM, France*
- Ruiling Feng, *Tianjin Normal University, China*
- Marta Fondo, *Universitat Oberta de Catalunya, Spain*
- Paula Fonseca, *Polytechnic Institute of Viseu, Portugal*
- Wendi Hulme, *Fanshawe College, Canada*
- José Luis Jiménez, *Catholic University Andrés Bello, Venezuela*

Notes on contributors

- Kristi Julian, *Middle Tennessee State University, United States*
- Ahmed Kharrufa, *Newcastle University, United Kingdom*
- Reinout Klamer, *The Hague University of Applied Sciences, Netherlands*
- Ilka Kressner, *University at Albany, United States*
- Ken Ludwig, *University of Michigan, United States*
- Maria De Lurdes Martins, *Polytechnic Institute of Viseu, Portugal*
- Catherine Muller, *Université Grenoble Alpes / LIDILEM, France*
- Kelly M. Murdoch-Kitt, *University of Michigan, United States*
- Elke Nissen, *Université Grenoble Alpes / LIDILEM, France*
- Catherine Roche, *Rockland Community, United States*
- Sheida Shirvani, *Ohio University, United States*
- Patricia Szobonya, *Rockland Community, United States*
- Alison Whelan, *Newcastle University, United Kingdom*

Introducing virtual exchange: towards digital equity in internationalisation

Müge Satar[1]

1. Background

The European Commission report (Helm & van der Velden, 2019) on the impact of Virtual Exchange (VE) on Higher Education (HE) students highlights the importance of VE in developing a wide range of skills, including 21st century skills, digital competences, soft skills such as teamwork, and collaborative problem solving, critical thinking, and media literacy. The report also evidences positive impact on perceived self-esteem, curiosity, intercultural sensitivity, reflection on beliefs and behaviours, and an ability to see complexity in intercultural communication. More recently, the value and role of VE in 'Internationalisation at Home' (IaH) has been foregrounded with an emphasis on the design of more environmentally sustainable, accessible, equitable, and meaningful intercultural and multinational experiences (Helm & Beaven, 2020). Improvement in employability skills and competences such as the ability to work in virtual, international, and intercultural environments has also been a key driver for recent VE projects (European Union and EACEA, 2020). The reduction in physical mobility opportunities due to the COVID-19 pandemic further increased interest in VE. But what is and what is not VE? How does VE support internationalisation agendas? What is the importance of digital equity in VE? This introductory chapter will attempt to briefly address these questions, and provide an overview of the organisation of this book which involves selected short papers presented at the International VE Conference (IVEC) 2020.

---

1. Newcastle University, Newcastle upon Tyne, United Kingdom; muge.satar@newcastle.ac.uk; https://orcid.org/0000-0002-2382-6740

How to cite: Satar, M. (2021). Introducing virtual exchange: towards digital equity in internationalisation. In M. Satar (Ed.), *Virtual exchange: towards digital equity in internationalisation* (pp. 1-13). Research-publishing.net. https://doi.org/10.14705/rpnet.2021.53.1285

Introduction

2. What is VE and what it is not?

"Virtual exchange is a pedagogical approach which involves the engagement of groups of learners in extended periods of online intercultural interaction and collaboration with partners from other cultural contexts or geographical locations as an integrated part of their educational programmes and under the guidance of educators and/or expert facilitators" (O'Dowd, 2020, p. 478).

Although VE is a relatively new term, it is not a new pedagogy. VE is also known as *telecollaboration, online intercultural exchange, Collaborative Online International Learning (COIL), international online learning,* and *globally networked learning,* among others (O'Dowd, 2018). While not everyone is completely happy with this new term, it is an attempt to bring together cross-disciplinary perspectives and promote wider cross-community collaboration and synergies (O'Dowd, 2021). Yet for the uninitiated, the term VE may not mean much since all educational exchanges in many countries were forced to take place virtually with the sudden impact of the COVID-19 pandemic in spring 2020. Thus, exploring what is *not* VE may also help clarify the concept for newcomers to the field.

First, while VE involves participants collaborating and learning from each other through online interaction, it is not 'distance education'. Distance education is an umbrella term for learning and teaching which takes place outside a physical classroom whereby students enrol in courses/programmes and work towards certificates and/or degrees offered by one or more institutions. Second, VE is not 'online teaching and learning' (or e-learning), which is one type of distance education where courses are offered online with digital delivery of materials, and interaction between teachers and learners taking place synchronously and/or asynchronously. Third, VE is not 'blended learning', which aims to combine online materials and interaction with teaching and learning within the classroom. Blended learning enables varying levels of physical and virtual presence, thus giving learners flexible amounts of control over where, when, and how to learn. Finally, VE is not 'virtual mobility'. Virtual mobility can be considered in comparison to physical mobility whereby HE students and teachers visit an overseas institution for a limited period to study or teach. An excellent example of physical mobility is the European Union Erasmus Programme for study abroad. Virtual mobility is then a response to widen opportunities for study abroad by enabling students and teachers to join teaching and learning at an overseas institution virtually without having to travel abroad. Yet VE is not an alternative to or replacement for physical mobility, with each generating equally valuable but different learning experiences.

VE can be incorporated and introduced as part of institutional programmes designed and delivered in the physical classroom, in distance education, online learning and teaching, or blended learning, or as tasks or modules for pre-mobility (Batardière et al., 2019; O'Reilly, 2021). Yet what distinguishes VE is that it focuses on the agency of the participants and highlights person-to-person digital engagement, interaction, and collaboration amongst intercultural groups of learners with the facilitation of their educators. The students continue to study at their own institutions, and their VE activities may be optional or compulsory as part of their programmes, and may or may not be assessed by their own institution.

3. VE, internationalisation, and digital equity in times of COVID-19

Internationalisation is "the process of integrating an international, intercultural or global dimension into the purpose, functions or delivery of post-secondary education" (Knight, 2003, p. 2). It responds to the need to offer global perspectives at HE and equip students with intercultural communication skills. Intercultural skills and competencies support HE graduates in their ability to interact and negotiate differences with people from various cultural backgrounds. Growing physical mobility in the last two decades amongst HE staff and students has increased the importance of internationalisation. More recently we have witnessed further interest in "the collaborative, mutual benefit, capacity building, and exchange aspects of internationalisation to optimise the benefit for individuals" (Knight, 2013, p. 84). Learning and practising intercultural competencies are essential to achieving these aspects of international education.

Internationalisation is a key strategic priority, yet, travel disruptions in the times of COVID-19 have really put the 'virtual' and 'digital' on top of internationalisation agendas at HE. VE and virtual mobility are sustainable and more accessible forms of mobility offering IaH to larger groups of staff and students. Previous studies have shown that VE can support meaningful interaction between learners of different lingua-cultural backgrounds (Dooly, 2017; O'Dowd & Lewis, 2016). The benefits of successful VE in the development of digital competences are also well established (Helm & van der Velden, 2019; Sadler & Dooly, 2016). Moreover, Hauck (2019) suggests that VE "offers an ideal backdrop" for the development of (critical) digital literacy skills (p. 205). Thus, VE is increasingly embraced by HE institutions as part of their IaH strategies.

However, digital intercultural communication in VE is "by default mediated twice" (Hauck & Satar, 2018, p. 133) by the technology and by the lingua franca and/or multiple languages used by the participants. On the one hand, technology enables VE participants to draw on a range of digital multimodal meaning-making resources and linguistic repertoires, thereby freeing them of the challenges experienced due to unequal linguistic competencies when communicating and collaborating with their intercultural peers. On the other hand, it poses new challenges to those who lack necessary 'digital' intercultural communication and semiotic competences. While VE as an approach to IaH seemingly offers equitable and accessible experiences to those who cannot participate in physical mobility, it is essential to remind ourselves that "online communication spaces [...] are not inherently equitable, and learners' varied levels of digital literacies, multimodal communicative competence, and semiotic skills tend to influence, if not determine, their VE experience" (Satar & Hauck, in press).

The theme for the IVEC 2020 conference was identified within this perspective which generated numerous high-quality presentations on the topic, some of which are reported in this volume.

4. IVEC 2020 and overview of this volume

This volume includes summaries of selected presentations from the second IVEC (2020)[2] virtually hosted at Newcastle University, UK. IVEC is the most prominent event in the discipline which brings together practitioners, administrative staff, educational leaders, researchers, instructional designers, and non-governmental organisations. Building on the success of the inaugural conference in 2019, IVEC 2020 widened participation and marked the convergence of VE networks and communities across the globe at a single event. It was an exciting event for UNICollaboration[3] members since the biannual UNICollaboration conference merged with IVEC at the IVEC 2020 conference. We welcomed 500 delegates from 47 countries with 90 pre-recorded presentations, 27 live workshops and symposia, and 14 highly-engaging networking sessions led by VE experts from the IVEC supporting institutions. Newcastle University Deputy Vice-Chancellor **Prof. Julie Sanders** opened the conference with a timely, eloquent speech. Thought-provoking keynote addresses by **Dr Mirjam Hauck**, from the Department of Languages at the Open University, and by **Prof. Thérèse Laferrière**, from the Faculty of Education Sciences at Université Laval in Quebec were warmly received. The recordings of the welcome speech and the keynote addresses are available on the IVEC website[4]. **Prof. Anita Patankar**, **Dr Maha Bali**, and **Dr Paulo Goes** closed the conference by offering their global VE perspectives in their well-received, inspiring panel discussion skillfully moderated by **Eva Haug**.

IVEC 2020 was planned as an on-site event taking place at Newcastle Upon Tyne, yet a difficult decision had to be made to hold the conference online as the impact of the COVID-19 pandemic on international travel became apparent. Sadly, the pandemic has brought great suffering to many around the world and tested – and perhaps built – our resilience, patience, and flexibility. While VE is not a new pedagogy for many, as physical mobility for education was

---

2. http://iveconference.org

3. https://www.unicollaboration.org/

4. http://iveconference.org/2020-conference/

Introduction

suspended due to the pandemic, we witnessed an exponential increase in interest and immediate need to connect students and educators across borders virtually. This pushed VE high on the internationalisation agenda at HE, which was at times perceived as the silver lining for the promotion and adoption of VE. The conference organising committee at Newcastle University and the IVEC 2020 steering committee were humbled by the high amount of interest and excellent feedback we received. I was both delighted and honoured to chair such an exciting, timely, and vibrant event.

The short papers reported in this book complement a special issue in the Journal of VE[5], which is also dedicated to selected manuscripts presented at IVEC 2020. The chapters address the conference theme 'towards digital equity in internationalisation' from the perspectives of students, educators, and administrators, and discuss the current state and future of online intercultural communication and collaborative learning. The volume is organised in four sub-themes: (1) the local and the global, (2) digital communication skills, (3) multisensory VE projects, and (4) staff and student voices. The chapters outline current pedagogy and research in VE by first providing an overview of project design and then reporting learner experiences and/or research outcomes.

4.1. The local and the global

The chapters in the first part report transnational and transdisciplinary VE projects that focus on local and global issues. First, **Patricia Szobonya** and **Catherine Roche** describe Generation Z students' engagement with local and global issues such as the United Nations Sustainable Development Goals, ethics, privacy, and sexuality. The authors illustrate how students explored and challenged these issues in three VEs organised between a community college in the USA and three countries: Morocco, China, and Iraq. The authors conclude that VE can be a welcoming environment for the young generation and help "make the world a better place for all citizens".

---

5. https://journal.unicollaboration.org/

Next, **Alun DeWinter** and **Reinout Klamer** describe an EU-funded project, iKudu, which aims to establish long-term COIL projects between five South African and five European universities. By setting up over 50 COIL exchanges during the lifetime of the project, the consortium members will establish relationships based on trust, co-creation, and co-equal partnerships, thereby bringing African perspectives to EU institutions and supporting decolonisation of the curricula as well as unpacking issues of diversity, equality, and north-south collaborations at HE through a decolonised lens.

In Chapter 3, **Paula Fonseca**, **Kristi Julian**, **Wendi Hulme**, **Maria De Lurdes Martins**, and **Regina Brautlacht** present opportunities and challenges in implementing multidisciplinary VE projects at HE. The authors report transversal skills students have gained through their intercultural, interdisciplinary exchanges including teamwork, teambuilding, and project management in international teams as they worked on environmental issues related to sustainability while contributing to discussions on global issues from their local and discipline-specific perspectives. The authors also elaborate on the challenges they encountered when designing and implementing interdisciplinary exchanges such as differences in syllabi, outcomes, and assessment.

Nadia Cheikhrouhou and **Kenneth Ludwig**, in Chapter 4, describe a USA-Tunisia exchange involving students from different disciplines, such as psychology, engineering, and computing working together to offer innovative solutions to water scarcity in the region of Khniss, Tunisia. While working on a local environmental problem in Tunisia, the authors describe how transdisciplinary teams developed transferable skills for life and work in global settings including critical thinking, problem solving, communication, teamwork, and information literacy skills. The teams had opportunities to reflect on availability of clean water as a global issue, and adopt a creative and flexible approach sensitive to various perspectives. On the other hand, the authors also report that at times some Tunisian students felt their American partners dominated the conversations which they attributed to their proficiency level in the language of the exchange, i.e. English.

4.2. Digital communication skills

The two chapters in the second part of this book zoom in on learners' linguistic competence and engage with issues around language and digital communication skills in VE. **Ruiling Feng** and **Sheida Shirvani** explore the uneven distribution of language proficiency amongst VE participants and elaborate on the different conversational strategies second language users adopt when communicating with VE partners who are first language users. The authors describe the compensatory strategies employed by Chinese learners of English during a five-week VE between China and the USA. Their findings indicate that second language learners used a variety of compensatory strategies depending on their conversational style and only corrected those errors in their language that interfered in meaning communication. The authors conclude that VE can support language learners' use of compensatory strategies with increased immediacy.

In Chapter 6, **Marta Fondo** explores visual communication via videoconferencing among Spanish and English speakers in four countries: Spain, Ireland, Mexico, and the USA. Fondo shows how language learners engaged in "visual supported actions (VSAs)", i.e. multimodal information exchange whereby learners show physical objects and other people to each other on camera during their online intercultural exchanges. Her findings indicate that participants achieved higher-levels of self-disclosure as they participated in visual communication through videoconferencing.

4.3. Multisensory VE projects

Chapters in the third part of this book direct our attention further to the visual in multisensory VE projects which require collaborative production of digital artefacts. In Chapter 7, **Kelly M. Murdoch-Kitt** and **Denielle J. Emans** describe a longitudinal VE between Middle East and North America over nine years in which participants engage in visual thinking activities producing 'boundary objects' such as sketches, photographs, and visualisations that generate shared understanding across cultural and disciplinary boundaries. The authors propose that the creation of boundary objects enhance relationship-building and trust, and offer tangible and tactile experiences to long-distance intercultural exchanges. They particularly promote visual communication activities to overcome barriers in lack of a common instructional language "to create more equitable, inclusive, and meaningful relationships".

In the next chapter, **Colin B. Dodds**, **Alison Whelan**, **Ahmed Kharrufa**, and **Müge Satar** describe a VE in which participants engage in the production of digital cultural artefacts on a web app[6] as they explore each other's cultural activities and identities. The exchange is designed within an experiential learning pedagogy in VE for future language teachers from two language teacher education programmes in Turkey and the UK. In this chapter, the authors describe the aims of the EU-funded project, the app design, and its implementation for VE as a model to "facilitate deeper, immersive virtual intercultural exchange experiences" and offer equitable, hands-on cultural experiences to all participants.

In the last chapter in Part 3, **José Luis Jiménez** and **Ilka Kressner** report their six-week task-based COIL project on expressions of popular culture between Venezuela and the USA. The project encourages learners to reflect on concepts and perceptions of popular culture in the North and the South through explorations of Indie music, graffiti, street art, and contemporary media. As the project culminated in a co-production of a ten-minute video, the authors observed how visual communication and collaboration led to "fostering empathy towards transcultural awareness and equitable collaboration".

4.4. Staff and student voices

The final three chapters in this book (Part 4), turn our attention to VE participants: staff and students. In Chapter 10, **Sofía Ruiz**, **Santiago Hernández**, **Alicia García**, and **Jesús Chacón** offer their learner voice as they describe their personal experiences of the USA-Venezuela VE explained in Chapter 9. They express learning gains from their exchange during – what they describe as – a time of crisis in Venezuela. Following an overview of the project, each author

---

6. www.enacteruopa.com

offers their individual perspective and the ways in which they managed to overcome challenges through their commitment, resilience, and agency.

In Chapter 11, **Elke Nissen**, **Catherine Felce**, and **Catherine Muller** report student expectations and outcomes identified through a large-scale survey as part of the Erasmus+ EVOLVE project with data originating from 16 VEs and 248 students. Their results indicate that VE outcomes are "unsurprisingly, more nuanced and manifold" than the initial expectations. While student expectations pertaining to intercultural gains largely match their perceived outcomes, students report unexpected gains in relation to transferable skills such as collaborative and communicative skills, which, the authors have found, are not always considered in course objectives.

The final chapter that concludes this volume focuses on the perspectives of HE staff considering both educators and administrators. **Ana Beaven** and **Gillian Davies** describe the structure of the Erasmus+ VE training offered to HE staff and illustrate how trainees developed their pedagogical, technical, and administrative VE skills and competencies through experiential learning. With highly positive responses received from the trainees, the authors remind us of the role of continuous professional development in VE since HE staff themselves may require experiential training to develop their own intercultural and digital communication skills as well as embracing new teaching practices to become successful VE facilitators for their students.

5.　Concluding remarks

Although VE is not a new pedagogy anymore, it has never been so timely and strong given the risks and restrictions in international travel due to the COVID-19 pandemic. Online/virtual connections ensured the continuity of intercultural interaction and mobility during an extremely challenging period for HE institutions. From the conversations that emerged during IVEC 2020, it is clear that HE institutions are ready for VE to become more mainstream, to provide brave spaces, and to break the online echo chambers. Yet, as Mirjam

Hauck argued in her keynote speech at IVEC 2020: "I want to warn against the superficial understanding of third space in virtual exchange because the digital spaces where most virtual exchanges take place are not neutral grounds; they are not necessarily levelling places". Thus, the challenge now is to ensure digital equity, social justice, diversity, and inclusion in VE, which, however, is not an easy task. As Satar and Hauck (in press) remind us:

> "[i]t is challenging for educators to ensure equal digital experiences for those involved in collaborative online learning and teaching communities such as VE. Equal access to technologies and the Internet, or – at least – a choice of accessible tools, is only one important precondition. In fact, equity in digital spaces, we conclude, is multifaceted and includes intercultural equity, participatory and relational equity, and semiotic equity, to name but a few of its dimensions".

As online and on-site transnational, transcultural interactions continue to merge and blend in, the papers in this volume suggest that we should expect to see an upward trend in the number of multinational, multidisciplinary VE projects, VE pedagogies that draw on visual communication, and digital artefacts to overcome barriers in linguistic challenges, as well as research focusing on the training needs, expectations, and outcomes of both staff and students partaking in VE.

6. Acknowledgements

I would like to express my sincere gratitude to the authors in this volume for their inspiring contributions on VE research and pedagogy. I would also like to thank the reviewers who kindly shared their collegial and critical comments with the authors to help improve the quality of this publication.

We are extremely pleased at Newcastle University to have had the opportunity to host IVEC 2020 with two excellent keynote speakers and a refreshing panel bringing in perspectives from around the world. It was a pleasure to work with the local organising committee at Newcastle University and the IVEC 2020 steering committee who generously shared their experience and advice in all aspects of the organisation. The IVEC 2020 Steering Committee consisted of representatives from the following institutions, and we are thankful for the time and effort they have invested in realising IVEC 2020: The State University of New York (SUNY) COIL Center, DePaul University, UNICollaboration, Drexel University, University of Washington Bothell, East Carolina University, Durban University of Technology, Universidad de Monterrey, Federal University of Pernambuco, and Newcastle University.

We are also grateful to the generous contributions of the conference sponsors: Newcastle University, Class2Class, and University of Washington Foster School of Business. Last but not least, the professionalism, efficiency, and thoroughness of Research-publishing.net ensured high-quality outcomes. I very much appreciate their contributions and support for the conference and the publication of this volume.

References

Batardière, M.-T., Giralt, M., Jeanneau, C., Le-Baron-Earle, F., & O'Regan, V. (2019). Promoting intercultural awareness among European university students via pre-mobility virtual exchanges. *Journal of Virtual Exchange, 2*, 1-6. https://doi.org/10.14705/rpnet.2019.jve.4

Dooly, M. (2017). Telecollaboration. In C. Chapelle & S. Sauro (Eds), *The handbook of technology and second language teaching* (pp. 169-182). Wiley.

European Union and EACEA. (2020). Erasmus+ Virtual Exchange – Handbook for international relations officers. https://europa.eu/youth/sites/default/files/eyp/eve/attachments/eve_-_handbook_for_iros_1.pdf

Hauck, M. (2019). Virtual exchange for (critical) digital literacy skills development. *European Journal of Language Policy, 11*(2), 187-211. https://doi.org/10.3828/ejlp.2019.12

Hauck, M., & Satar, H. M. (2018). Learning and teaching languages in technology-mediated contexts: the relevance of social presence, co-presence, participatory literacy and multimodal competence. In R. Kern & C. Develotte (Eds), *Screens and scenes: online multimodal communication and intercultural encounters: theoretical and educational perspectives* (pp. 133-157). Routledge. https://doi.org/10.4324/9781315447124-7

Helm, F., & Beaven, A. (2020). (Eds). *Designing and implementing virtual exchange – a collection of case studies*. Research-publishing.net. https://doi.org/10.14705/rpnet.2020.45.9782490057726

Helm, F., & van der Velden, B. (2019). Erasmus+ Virtual Exchange Intercultural learning experiences: 2018 impact report. European Union and EACEA. https://europa.eu/youth/sites/default/files/eyp/eve/attachments/181025_eve_-_preliminary_impact_review_jan-june_2018__1.pdf

Knight, J. (2003). Updated internationalization definition. *International Higher Education, 33*, 2-3.

Knight, J. (2013). The changing landscape of higher education internationalisation – for better or worse? *Perspectives: Policy and Practice in Higher Education, 17*(3), 84-90. https://doi.org/10.1080/13603108.2012.753957

O'Dowd, R. (2018). From telecollaboration to virtual exchange: state-of-the-art and the role of UNICollaboration in moving forward. *Journal of Virtual Exchange, 1*, 1-23. https://doi.org/10.14705/rpnet.2018.jve.1

O'Dowd, R. (2020). A transnational model of virtual exchange for global citizenship education. *Language Teaching, 53*(4), 477-490. https://doi.org/10.1017/s0261444819000077

O'Dowd, R. (2021). Virtual exchange: moving forward into the next decade. *Computer Assisted Language Learning, 34*(3), 209-224. https://doi.org/10.1080/09588221.2021.1902201

O'Dowd, R., & Lewis, T. (2016). (Eds). *Online intercultural exchange: policy, pedagogy, practice*. Routledge studies in language and intercultural communication. Routledge.

O'Reilly, C. (2021). Reflection on practice: an exploration of a virtual online collaboration as preparation for the year abroad. *Journal of Virtual Exchange, 4*, 50-61. https://doi.org/10.21827/jve.4.35781

Sadler, R., & Dooly, M. (2016). Twelve years of telecollaboration: what we have learnt. *Elt Journal, 70*(4), 401-413. https://doi.org/10.1093/elt/ccw041

Satar, M., & Hauck, M. (in press). Exploring digital equity in online learning communities (virtual exchange). In D. Kelly & A. de Medeiros (Eds), *Language debates in the language acts and worldmaking series*. John Murray Languages.

Section 1.
The local and the global

1 Intercultural youth: the global generation and virtual exchange

Patricia Szobonya[1] and Catherine Roche[2]

Abstract

Due to the interconnectedness of our world and the ubiquitous presence of technology, it is imperative that students be introduced to and be actively involved in cross-cultural activities. Generation Z (Gen Z) students have been raised with computer-based technology; and as a result, they are cognizant of social and global issues that transcend borders and require collaborative solutions. Collaborative Online International Learning (COIL) and other virtual exchange programs provide students with the opportunity to engage in real conversations and problem solving with students from other countries. Students connect asynchronously and/or synchronously to discuss, analyze, and solve problems together. Simplified short-term projects also have relevance as they provide the opportunity for communication leading to empathy and awareness of social and economic injustices around the world. While study abroad is considered a traditional method of introducing students to other cultures, most students do not have the time nor the financing to be able to travel. However, today virtual exchange empowered by technology is a viable, sustainable method. In this contribution, examples of tasks, activities, technologies, and challenges resulting from various collaborations around the globe, in particular with Morocco, Iraq, and China, are highlighted. Through these collaborations, students established personal connections and shared responsibility in addressing local and global concerns.

1. Rockland Community, Suffern, New York, USA; pszobony@sunyrockland.edu; https://orcid.org/0000-0003-4655-313X

2. Rockland Community, Suffern, New York, USA; croche@sunyrockland.edu; https://orcid.org/0000-0003-1562-8899

How to cite: Szobonya, P., & Roche, C. (2021). Intercultural youth: the global generation and virtual exchange. In M. Satar (Ed.), *Virtual exchange: towards digital equity in internationalisation* (pp. 17-28). Research-publishing.net. https://doi.org/10.14705/rpnet.2021.53.1286

Chapter 1

> All of the collaborations underscore the value of virtual exchange activities, transcontinental partnerships, and collective action. The global pandemic has fostered the opportunity to explore more of these enriching exchanges.

Keywords: Generation Z, technology, virtual exchange, global, collaboration, digital divide.

1. Introduction

This paper will discuss Gen Z and their participation in virtual exchange. It will also highlight the value of adding a virtual exchange to enrich the higher education curriculum. Examples of virtual exchanges will showcase the student experience between Rockland Community College (RCC) and various institutions around the world.

Previous generations around the globe have displayed different characteristics, behaviors, and attitudes unique to their cultural environment. While this is true for Gen Z, they have the added attribute of being the first true global generation (Rapacon, 2019). This unique generation has come of age in an already technologically empowered world, with accessibility to information in real time. Information that is rapidly updated on 24-hour news cycles, coupled with the ubiquity of mobile devices, make Gen Z one of the most well-informed generations. They have taken up the challenge that their predecessors, the millennials, have initiated in recognizing and solving common global problems such as those identified in the United Nations[3]; 17 Sustainable Development Goals addressing the issues of *hunger, poverty, health, education, gender equality, clean water, clean energy, decent work, industry innovation and infrastructure, inequality, sustainable cities and communities, responsible consumption and production, climate action, life below water, life on land, peace and justice,*

---

3. https://sdgs.un.org/goals

and lastly *partnerships to achieve the goal*. Gen Z is on the brink of maturity, cognizant of these worldwide issues and equipped with the tech savvy skills and determination to build partnerships around the world. Along with guidance from their respective professors, virtual exchange interactions provide students with the opportunity to develop meaningful conversations with like-minded students around the world. In this paper, collaborations that have occurred between our institution in New York, RCC, and institutions in the Middle East and China will be described.

2. Gen Z activism

Gen Z has inspired activism throughout the world, notably in the current Black Lives Matter movement, sparked by the death of George Floyd by a Minneapolis police officer last spring (Hill et al., 2020). This event would set forth in motion one of the largest movements in history propelled by Gen Z (Bellan, 2020). At the grassroots level, this young generation used social media posts on various platforms such as Instagram, Twitter, and TikTok to raise awareness and to communicate and connect with empathizing participants (Parker & Igielnik, 2020). Also, another historical event, in 2019, a million students around the world followed 16-year-old Swedish student, Greta Thunberg, and walked out of classes to protest inaction on climate change (Burr, 2020). This generation is in classrooms today throughout the world – the generation that will continue their education in the coming years to prepare for career opportunities.

3. Characteristics of Gen Z

Using 1996 as the birth year for Gen Z renders the oldest members 25 years old. Without any memory of a disconnected world, they are true digital natives, even more than their predecessors, the millennials. Each generation experiences events that are unique to them and shape their view of the world. Gen Z has experienced not only recessions but economic downturns intensified by the pandemic as well as several geopolitical conflicts resulting in international tensions.

The unique traits of Gen Z students make them ideal candidates for virtual exchange opportunities. Collaborative activities conducted through various e-platforms enable students to communicate, conduct critical analysis, and become aware of real-world problems with other students across the globe. Problems are no longer localized; through technology, students are aware of global concerns and injustices. Collaborations can underscore social problems, sustainability issues, and develop cultural empathy through the lens of intercultural awareness and understanding.

4. Gen Z and higher education

Gen Z's enrollment in higher education surpasses the enrollment of previous generations (Parker & Igielnik, 2020). Their perspective on college is viewed as a means to an end or as a gateway to world readiness (Mintz, 2019). Gen Z students are entrepreneurial, desire practical skills in their education, and are concerned not only about the realization of social injustices but also the ability to make change (Schroeder, 2020).

To address this goal, faculty should design curricula that prepare students and address their career ambitions, open windows to various career options, and incorporate more authentic, real-world projects into classes (Mintz, 2019). Traditionally, experiential learning activities have been conducted in the physical workplace. However, these activities cannot be simply abandoned now due to current limitations of the COVID-19 pandemic but must be adapted to the virtual environment. Since education has transitioned to the virtual world, so must experiential learning experiences.

RCC, one of 64 institutions in the State University of New York system of higher education, joined the COIL network in 2014. During the past six years, faculty have participated in professional development workshops and partnering activities in preparation to offer virtual international experiences to their students. Faculty in the Art, Business, English, Hospitality, Legal Studies, Multicultural Studies, Political Science, Science, and Speech Departments have developed and delivered collaborations with partners in various countries. Most of these collaborations have been sustained throughout the years involving the same COIL partners. Partners continually update their collaborations by introducing new ideas, projects, and technological tools. Initially faculty used tools such as a closed Facebook group and Skype; however, more recently Zoom, Slack, Flipgrid, and WhatsApp among other applications have been utilized for communication. The following examples will showcase some experiences from RCC professors and their partnering institutions.

4.1. Examples of virtual exchange – Morocco

Inclusive collaborations unite students across the world and allow for discussions of global problems as identified by the 17 UN Sustainable Development Goals. In the Fall of 2019, a collaboration with Mohammed Premier University (UMP), Oujda, Morocco, and RCC examined the influences of young people and what encouraged them to join political, social, or at times radical movements. In RCC, 20 students were enrolled in an Intro to Multicultural Studies course and paired with approximately 20 students from an English course in UMP. All students initially introduced themselves via video or photos with corresponding text in a private Facebook group, describing their interests and studies, along with the best and worst thing about living in their country. This was the icebreaker, intended to formulate trust and foster community building. The second task was to compare concerns unique to their countries that create cause for such movements.

Students discovered that both countries were confronted with multiple layers of oppression that involved political, environmental, and societal constraints. For example, many students from RCC suggested that discrimination was a crucial issue, also climate change, and the political divide in the US. UMP students more often concluded religious discrimination was paramount to other issues. The students analyzed the intersectional challenges that inspired movements. Other issues recognized as typical motivators were the lack of financial security, the need for basic human rights, and governmental bureaucracy. UMP students noted that the youth in Morocco had little opportunities of engagement or activities, where joining movements offered defining moments to fight negative social phenomena. Some students at RCC claimed that youth in the US were indifferent at times, but also suggested that youth are keen to the mistakes of past generations and highly motivated for change. Protesting is an active way for youth to contribute to the cause.

Student groups considered methods for societies that would encourage inclusivity for youth. Some group suggestions were to lower the voting age so that youth had a voice, create additional youth programs, continue to educate, and lastly for adults to actively listen and boost the morale of youth.

Another collaboration with UMP in Fall 2017 focused on courses in different disciplines. The Moroccan students were enrolled in English Fourth Year of Civil Engineering within the module of Langues et Communication, and the US students at RCC were enrolled in Principles of Management, a required course for business majors. Despite the disparity in subject matter, partners established common ground enabling both to achieve their respective course objectives. In Principles of Management, global business, cross-cultural communication, and human resources were the topics selected to pursue in the collaboration. The Moroccan course focused on professional writing in English for students preparing for careers in engineering. Since this project was awarded a Steven's Initiative grant, partners were trained in person in Lebanon and then traveled to Morocco for further discussion and planning of the collaboration. Partners determined that the following outcomes would align well with the disparate courses.

- Learning Outcome 1: explore cultural differences and similarities between Morocco and the United States.

- Learning Outcome 2: examine cross-cultural communication patterns regarding employment documents and practices.

Students were involved in an icebreaker activity, 'what would you do' scenarios, and then a final project in which they commented on each other's employment documents. For the 'what would you do' tasks, students were presented with various real-life scenarios and were asked to react. In one scenario, students were told that they were on their way to a very important job interview, the job of their dreams. On the way to the interview, however, they met a close friend who was very upset and experiencing a personal crisis. The friend wanted to talk right away. However, if the student stopped to listen and to console the friend, the student would undoubtedly miss the bus and be late for the important job interview. Students were asked what they would do in this situation.

For the most part, the American students reacted in a manner that demonstrated their individual orientation. Although they did care about their friend, their personal priority was getting to the interview on time. After the interview, they would speak to their friend.

Conversely, most of the Moroccan students demonstrated a more collective style. They offered to stay with the friend or even asked a family member to take care of the friend while they were at the interview. Student reactions revealed behavior that was consistent with one of Hofstede's dimensions of culture, collectivism versus individualism[4].

4.2. Virtual exchange – China

In the Fall and Spring of 2019, synchronous collaborations were conducted with students in a business course at Nanjing University, Nanjing, China, and students in a History of Multiculturism in American Business course at RCC. Each course had approximately 20 students. Students were placed in small groups where they met once a week for six weeks, using Skype as a platform to communicate. The main challenge for these collaborations was the time difference. Partners agreed that the students in China would return to their classroom at 11:00 pm, while the students in the United States would begin class at 8:00 am. For the first weekly activity, conducted live through Skype, the students analyzed and compared China's *social* credit score with the *financial* credit score used in the United States. Students considered the benefits, disadvantages, and ethical issues

---

[4]. https://www.hofstede-insights.com/

Chapter 1

of using a score. Students determined that while the scores in both countries had similar uses, there were concerns for privacy, ethics, and discrimination. Another topic discussed included sexual orientation provided by a guest lecturer who presented to both classes utilizing Skype. Students discussed various ways people identify in regard to sexuality and gender. The level of acceptance was also compared within each country. In the US most students raised their hand when asked if they knew someone who identified as gay. The number of hands raised from the students in China was significantly less. The students in China consider sexual orientation to be a private matter. The next activity involved the family structure and dynamics, where students considered the western influence in China. In China, more students had lived with their grandparents, and their grandparents were also the most respected. In the US, some students lived with their grandparents, but the breadwinner held the most respect. In each collaboration, it was realized that traditional values and roles continue to be prominent in China, more so than the United States.

4.3. Virtual exchange – Iraq

The Global Solutions Sustainability Challenge[5] is a virtual exchange initiative that promotes career readiness in the United States, Iraq, and Jordan. The program is supported by the Stevens Initiative[6] and administered by the Aspen Institute. IREX (International Research and Exchanges Board) is an independent nonprofit organization dedicated to building a more inclusive world by empowering youth, cultivating leaders, and extending access to quality education and information[7].

During Spring 2020, teams from RCC and Anbar University in Iraq worked together to identify a common problem relating to the broad topic of sustainability and to create a business solution. Teams brainstormed ideas in class before attending Zoom sessions. During these virtual sessions, the misconceptions and inaccurate stereotypical accounts that are often portrayed by the media were

---

5. https://www.irex.org/project/global-solutions

6. https://www.stevensinitiative.org/

7. https://www.diasporaengager.com/public/pdirectory/directory.php?

revealed and ultimately dispelled. By learning about life and the daily challenges faced by citizens in both countries, students were able to empathize and extract shared problems while becoming cognizant of problems indigenous to one country or the other.

Due to the global pandemic, both institutions were forced to transition to remote learning for the remainder of the project. Because of school shutdowns, both teams were asked if they would like to continue the challenge. When relying on technology available only at home, several Iraqi students were unable to continue as they did not have online access. However, the US students transitioned more easily to remote learning, and Slack, Zoom, and Google Drive became an integral element of remote learning. Since the collaboration was online, students were already accustomed to using Slack and Zoom to communicate with partners in Iraq. However, now these applications were also used for class meetings. Teamwork became even more crucial as the opportunity to be in one room in a face-to-face environment was no longer possible. Despite this extra challenge upon a challenge, the students continued to engage in problem solving, decision making, and negotiation skills. The result was a bi-country perspective on sustainability, familiarity with the human design process, and a firsthand experience with understanding and practicing empathy. Some of the comments in the post-collaboration reflection revealed increased student interest in sustainability issues, engineering, and learning Arabic.

5. Inequality in education revealed

COVID-19 has demonstrated the interconnectedness of our world. It does not discriminate and has demanded paradigm shifts in our daily lives. Education is one of several sectors that has been deeply affected by the pandemic, revealing an even wider digital divide than previously acknowledged. The inherent inequities of education at all levels around the globe have become apparent as institutions rapidly transitioned to online, remote, and other newly created modes of digital learning. Virtual modes require specific hardware and/or software, a dependable Internet connection, faculty preparation and training, and proper student habits such as self-discipline and time management. Lack of funding sources that would provide the necessary equipment and support as previously mentioned will contribute to an even larger divide with continuing inequities.

Since last spring, many faculty members have continued conducting classes remotely. Although this transition was not welcome by all students and faculty at the time, it was necessary. However, on the positive side, opportunities for virtual exchange and international partnerships became apparent. COVID-19 may be a positive black swan moment for higher education – just the impetus necessary to explore international collaborations (Mazzoleni, Turchetti, & Ambrosino, 2020).

Even prior to the pandemic, only a small percentage of community college students participated in study abroad programs. Time and financial constraints make it very difficult for them to take advantage of direct immersion in another culture through travel. Study abroad is the traditional method for introducing students to other cultures and has served to internationalize a course or curriculum; however, the pandemic has temporarily discontinued this traditional applied learning experience. As the world slowly returns to a new normal, many business practices and educational pedagogies will be reexamined. No doubt study abroad will be critically evaluated to determine its return on investment. Will the persistent anxiety regarding safety protocols and travel be worth the time, effort, expense, and possible risk involved? Can the objectives of a study abroad program be achieved through virtual exchange? Can virtual exchange achieve objectives that study abroad cannot?

Countries will continue to face challenges in terms of virus surges, testing, contact tracing, and vaccine availability and distribution. Closed borders and possible quarantines can wreak havoc on a carefully planned study abroad trip, especially one of short duration. In addition, the same constraints regarding study abroad are still apparent in a post-pandemic environment. For example, even if a student could afford to travel in pre-pandemic days, parents may not be able to finance a trip now due to lost jobs with ensuing high rates of unemployment.

For the time being, remote learning continues at home, but students do miss social interactions on and off campus. Although they fully understand the reasons for remote learning, the feelings of isolation and disconnectedness still prevail. Virtual exchange can address this issue through technology – connecting students on an interpersonal, human level. Virtual exchange is not a substitute for study abroad but simply another vehicle by which the playing field can become more level resulting in greater equity for all. Increasing numbers of students should have the chance to discuss and explore global issues with their peers in institutions around the world, resulting in awareness and possibly even viable solutions.

6. Conclusion

Gen Z and their future is somewhat on hold as international education opportunities are limited due to travel restrictions. Many countries are still not accepting visitors due to the spread of new COVID variants and low vaccination rates. Although this picture may appear bleak, it does present a perfect time for virtual exchange. As mentioned previously, virtual exchange has the power to level the playing field by giving all students the opportunity to work with students from other cultures. Students who were not able to travel even before the pandemic will be able to travel virtually and be connected with peers around the globe. Virtual exchange can unite this cohort of budding activists to come together in a welcoming, educative environment to make the world a better place for all citizens.

References

Bellan, R. (2020, June 12). Gen Z leads the black lives matter movement, on and off social media. *Forbes*. http://www.forbes.com/sites/rebeccabellan/2020/06/12/gen-z-leads-the-black-lives-matter-movement-on-and-off-social-media/

Burr, T. (2020, October 23). Portrait of a young climate activist in 'I Am Greta'. *The Boston Globe*. https://www.bostonglobe.com/2020/10/23/arts/portrait-young-climate-activist-i-am-greta/

Hill, E., Tiefenthäler, A., Triebert, C., Jordan, D., Willis, H., & Stein, R. (2020, June 1). How George Floyd was killed in police custody. *The New York Times.* https://www.nytimes.com/2020/05/31/us/george-floyd-investigation.html?auth=login-facebook

Mazzoleni, S., Turchetti, G., & Ambrosino, N. (2020). The COVID-19 outbreak: from "black swan" to global challenges and opportunities. *Pulmonology, 26*(3), 117-118. https://doi.org/10.1016/j.pulmoe.2020.03.002

Mintz, S. (2019, March 18). Are colleges ready for Generation Z? *inside higher ed.* https://www.insidehighered.com/blogs/higher-ed-gamma/are-colleges-ready-generation-z

Parker, K., & Igielnik, R. (2020, October 19). *What we know about Gen Z so far.* Pew Research Center's Social & Demographic Trends Project. https://www.pewsocialtrends.org/essay/on-the-cusp-of-adulthood-and-facing-an-uncertain-future-what-we-know-about-gen-z-so-far/

Rapacon, S. (2019, July 11). Gen Z's tech-driven take on adulting. *The Garage.* https://garage.hp.com/us/en/modern-life/generation-z-redefining-the-world.html

Schroeder, B. (2020, February 18). A majority of Gen Z aspires to be entrepreneurs and perhaps delay or skip college. Why that might be a good idea. *Forbes.* https://www.forbes.com/sites/bernhardschroeder/2020/02/18/a-majority-of-gen-z-aspires-to-be-entrepreneurs-and-perhaps-delay-or-skip-college-why-that-might-be-a-good-idea/

2 Can COIL be effective in using diversity to contribute to equality? Experiences of iKudu, a European-South African consortium operating via a decolonised approach to project delivery

Alun DeWinter[1] and Reinout Klamer[2]

Abstract

The iKudu project is a north-south collaboration between five universities in South Africa and five in Europe. As an EU-funded project, the overall aim is to capacity build around internationalisation at home through Collaborative Online International Learning (COIL). Originally presented at IVEC2020, this paper explores how iKudu navigates and utilises concepts of equality, equity through decolonisation, and Africanisation. Drawing from experiences of the first year of operation, this paper presents how the iKudu project was designed with equality in mind in order to ensure that as many students can engage in internationalisation activities, but notes how the realities of decolonisation introduce challenging contradictions for the consortium to navigate, particularly around the use of the English language in a global context. This paper also presents some of the underlying working philosophies from the perspective of the iKudu leadership to show just how COIL can be effective in contributing to equality within internationalisation of Higher Education (HE).

Keywords: COIL, international, partnership, collaboration, equality, decolonisation.

1. Coventry University, Coventry, United Kingdom; aa2567@coventry.ac.uk; https://orcid.org/0000-0002-0978-7482

2. The Hague University of Applied Sciences, The Hague, Netherlands; h.r.klamer@hhs.nl; https://orcid.org/0000-0002-7114-6133

How to cite: DeWinter, A., & Klamer, R. (2021). Can COIL be effective in using diversity to contribute to equality? Experiences of iKudu, a European-South African consortium operating via a decolonised approach to project delivery. In M. Satar (Ed.), *Virtual exchange: towards digital equity in internationalisation* (pp. 29-40). Research-publishing.net. https://doi.org/10.14705/rpnet.2021.53.1287

Chapter 2

1. Introduction

iKudu[3] is a current Erasmus+ funded capacity building project which involves five South African and five European universities[4] in establishing long term north-south COIL projects. COIL projects are designed to bring together learners from geographically distant institutions in order to undertake a meaningful collaborative activity that encourages global engagement and develops intercultural competences. Importantly, this form of internationalisation can be achieved 'from home' and without physical mobility (SUNY COIL, 2020). iKudu is designed to contribute to developing a contextualised South African concept of internationalisation of the curriculum and bringing an African perspective to the curricula of the European partner institutions.

The consortium itself is diverse: within the ten institutions, there are research-focused universities, universities of technology, and universities of applied sciences. There is also an element of inequity to navigate, with certain institutions located in less affluent areas, with limited access to technology. Within the lens of COIL, consortium partner universities differ in their experiences of internationalisation at home; certain institutions have a long history of embedding COIL into their teaching and learning, whereas others are just starting out on this journey.

The intended curriculum transformation through COIL includes a strong focus on Africanisation and decolonisation through a spirit of co-creation and co-equal partnerships. In total, the project aims to set up over 50 COIL projects between Europe and South Africa, to serve as a foundation for long term opportunities.

This paper focuses on these concepts of diversity and equality, and how north-south collaborations can utilise COIL when navigating issues of

---

3. https://www.ufs.ac.za/ikudu/

4. iKudu consortium partners are: South Africa (University of Free State, Durban University of Technology, Central University of Technology, University of Venda, and University of Limpopo) and Europe (Coventry University, The Hague University of Applied Sciences, University of Siena, University of Antwerp, and Amsterdam University of Applied Sciences). References: Agyekum (2018); Almeida, Robson, Morosini, and Baranzeli (2019); Cooperrider, Whitney, and Stavros (2008); De Wit, Hunter, Howard, and Egron-Polak (2015); Esche (2018); IESA (2004); Liyange (2020); Molefe (2016); Nzimande (2017).

internationalisation at home through a decolonised lens. Drawing from existing literature and initial interview evidence with key iKudu stakeholders, this paper starts by exploring the concepts of equality and decolonisation in a north-south context. Further experiences of iKudu stakeholders will then be presented before offering conclusions as to how COIL can contribute to equality within the internationalisation of HE.

2. Why COIL?

Internationalisation in HE is widely accepted as "the intentional process of integrating an international, intercultural or global dimension into the purpose, functions and delivery of post-secondary education, in order to enhance the quality of education and research for all students and staff, and to make a meaningful contribution to society" (De Wit, Hunter, Howard, & Egron-Polak, 2015, p. 283). However, internationalisation practices within HE have been criticised for being elitist, particularly with travel abroad being economically prohibitive for many students around the world (De Wit et al., 2015).

From the South African perspective, internationalisation has been an area of growing concern for over the past two decades, with the need to join up national policy and institutional practice being seen as a priority due to a perceived disconnect between the two (IESA, 2004). More recently, the South African Government has moved to draft policy to embed internationalisation, particularly through internationalisation at home, noting that overseas mobility presents an inherent limitation for South African institutions (Nzimande, 2017).

This idea of access for all was integral to the design of iKudu. During an interview conducted on August 25th 2020, Cornelius Hagenmeier, Chair of the iKudu consortium, noted:

> "the specific focus on internationalisation and COIL is a logical consequence of our focus to develop internationalisation in such a way that allows all students to participate. Traditionally when

internationalisation was based on participation to those who could afford to travel and the few who were excellent enough to be funded. Its benefit was limited to a small group of people".

During an interview conducted on August 25th 2020, Merle Hodges, iKudu consultant also notes:

"we as a South African HE system, feel that is it very important to internationalize, we want to impart of the world's knowledge production, we want to contribute to the SDGs [the United Nations Sustainable Development Goals] and develop our students with the necessary student attributes of employability, of critical thinking, of transdisciplinary thinking, so that they can become participants in the world arena".

The iKudu project therefore focuses on COIL as a form of internationalisation at home, due to the limited possibilities for other forms of traditional mobility within the north-south collaborative context. This helps ensure equality of access to students from all ten institutions. Indeed, internationalisation at home is seen as an approach that allows institutions in the global south to build capacity in HE and to challenge the hegemony of universities in the north (Almeida et al., 2019).

Within iKudu, the use of COIL also allows for a greater sense of democratisation within internationalisation and places focus on the specific local context of each university. Operating in an online space, ownership and creation of the COIL is designed to be 'co-equal' and should not be dominated by any one partner. In the spirit of co-equal partnering and decision-making, effort is shared, rather than dictated. Every institution is the expert in their own local context and this experience and expertise should be incorporated into the COIL design and delivery. Therefore, the diversity found within these institutions directly feeds into the rich intercultural exchange that COIL fosters as part of the international collaboration.

That being said, despite the clear benefits that COIL offers in terms of offering equality within internationalisation within HE, through offering internationalisation at home without the need to spend on travel, things do get more complex when issues relating to equity and decolonisation are considered. Van Hove (2019) notes that COIL exchanges are not simply a 'cheap and easy' way of delivering internationalisation and instead requires much thought and effort in terms of design and delivery to make the collaboration truly meaningful.

3. Navigating decolonisation

Decolonisation is an incredibly emotive issue, not least due to the difficult realities of the colonial legacy experienced in South Africa throughout the 20th and 21st century. South Africa is a world leader in challenging educational practices through decolonisation, with campaigns appearing from 2015 to pluralise education and to challenge "the domination of Western epistemological traditions, histories and figures" (Molefe, 2016, p. 32). This has gradually influenced European universities to reconsider their own approaches to HE, with Liyange (2020) labelling systemic racial inequality in HE as a 'silent crisis' in the UK and Europe.

Decolonisation can be seen as a 'levelling up' of the equality agenda, moving beyond equality of access to concepts of equity and truly co-equal partnership within HE. One of COIL's greatest strengths is that it is accessible to a larger pool of participants, particularly those who cannot engage with physical international mobility, and that COIL activity is strengthened through the diversity of its partners (De Wit, 2013, p. 1). That being said, issues of inequity do present themselves in COIL activity and it is within this decolonised space that iKudu is seeking to have meaningful impact.

The iKudu steering committee has taken steps to help enshrine a decolonised, Africanised approach to the project, with two working groups being created to help deliver all elements of the project. It is also important to note that, although this is an EU-funded project, project leadership is actually South African, with Cornelius Hagenmeier leading from the University of The Free State. Workgroup 1 focuses on researching the status of internationalisation of the curriculum of the different partners involved and advising how these universities can best reach their own aims. Workgroup 2 focuses on developing the framework and trainings to realise the COIL collaborations between the universities. Both workgroups have equal representation from the northern and the southern institutions, promoting this idea of co-equal creation and allowing all stakeholders to influence and shape the project content.

During an interview conducted on August 25th 2020, Hodges stated:

> "when the iKudu project was formed, we looked at what is the government going to do and how does the government see HE within the African context. I quote from our national development plan: 'we are Africans, we are an African country, we are part of a multinational region, we are essential part of the continent, and we are acutely aware of the wider world and deeply implicated in our past and in our present. We want to have equal education and equal opportunity by the end of 2030'".

Despite the considered approach to iKudu project design and delivery, COIL itself presents two notable contradictions to decolonised practice. The first of these relates to English as the *lingua franca,* which Agyekum (2018) sees as 'linguistic imperialism', particularly in an Africanised context (p. 87). This is an unfortunate reality for globalised projects and one that iKudu is unable to fully address within the scope of the project. Although COIL activity within iKudu is delivered in English, this is perhaps one area that needs careful reflection on when considering the future of COIL through a decolonised lens.

The second contradiction relates to the delivery of staff training. Esche (2018) notes that the use of online learning is a traditionally western approach and indeed, in terms of length of experience, it is generally the European partners within the consortium who are taking the lead in the staff training, with the South African partners becoming the trainees. Although this may be viewed as an inherent flaw, iKudu is committed to ensuring that training serves as a baseline for activity, with Africanisation (and the challenging of northern models of education) being put at the centre of the COIL activity so that decolonisation can be made integral to the capacity building going forwards.

Despite the existence of these challenges, all members of the consortium are committed to enshrining the spirit of decolonisation and Africanisation through iKudu and are striving to harness the inherent diversity within all of the stakeholders. This paper will now offer a snapshot of the experiences of some of these stakeholders from project activity to date.

4. iKudu in practice

As we have seen, the iKudu project was designed with equality and decolonisation in mind, with a focus on creating this equal opportunity for all students. This was also reflected in practice by the project consortium chair Hagenmeier's iKudu philosophy, which focuses on international collaboration processes and capacity building:

> "we consider Africanisation, internationalisation and decolonisation as a complementary process. The question is not with whom you collaborate but how you collaborate. […] So this idea of equality, of using the existing diversity and to build up relationships between continents that were once colonizer and colonized was placed at the heart of the project. Internationalisation should be for everyone and these COIL projects can help to achieve these central ideas. With specific attention for capacitating academics to deliver an international viewpoint on internationalisation" (Interview conducted on August 25th 2020).

During an interview conducted on August 25th, 2020, iKudu consultant Hodges reinforced this idea of capacity building especially with an emphasis on transdisciplinarity:

> "this is what the COIL projects can do, to assist our academics, to improve their teaching and learning skills, their technological skills but also to

> improve their knowledge base, to make this more transdisciplinary, because our students need this critical thinking, they must communicate and collaborate and these are the skills needed in the new normal, after the pandemic".

The initial vision for delivery was impacted by the COVID 2020 crisis, and resulted in all training and development activity to move into an online space. As a result, only a limited number of projects have been completed to date but many projects are scheduled between September 2020 and January 2022. This activity was originally planned to take place between March and July 2020, when COVID cases were rising rapidly in Europe and institutions were preoccupied with transforming their existing courses to an online environment. Despite this setback, there are more than 20 projects planned for the period until January 2022, involving over 40 academics from all ten universities, from different educational fields. The process of partnering academics, delivering training, running the COIL projects, and evaluating these projects is done in a collaborative atmosphere, with workload shared across the consortium. Diversity is not only between South Africa and Europe but also interdisciplinary. Often the partnered academics work in cross-disciplinary COIL projects, where there is no direct match between the academic fields. This can provide new insights.

The experiences of academics that have already completed COIL projects are positive about iKudu. During an interview on the 28th September 2020, one Dutch academic reflected on their positive experience of transdisciplinary collaboration:

> "I was very interested in the field of the other academic, I thought how can we as a marketing lecturer and a nutrition researcher bring these fields together. Our students would do research on nutritional guidelines, but also interview each other, each other's food habits and the marketing side was focusing on the food trends and focusing on some sort of advice. That is how we combined the fields together, that is how we just loved it".

During an interview on the 28th September 2020, their South African partner academic confirmed this perspective and said: "the beauty is that it is cross disciplinary and really combines the different fields of expertise".

Also, the issues of diversity and how this was observed during the COVID-19 pandemic were addressed in the course. During an interview on the 28th September 2020, the Dutch academic noted: "this project took place during the pandemic, I made my students clear that in some countries the Coronavirus hits students harder, the students in South Africa might be more affected by this".

We can also observe that both academics focused on diversity and on intercultural sensitivity, specifically on letting the students reflect on their own culture, again demonstrating the innate ability of COIL to promote equality through sharing. During an interview on the 28th September 2020, the Dutch academic reflected on how their students may sometimes be perceived by students from other cultures as follows: "from previous projects with other countries we hear that Dutch students are sometimes seen as arrogant, as not really interested, be aware of this".

On the other hand, during the interview on the 28th September 2020, the South African partner highlighted that there are not only differences, but also sometimes surprising similarities between the students from each partner institution: "my students are surprised by the many similarities, the European students are very similar to us, like the same music, have similar topics and interest".

Another element which reinforces the foundation of equality in practice is the research work undertaken by iKudu's Workgroup 1. An appreciative enquiry is currently being undertaken in order to discover how internationalisation of the curriculum works in each context, across the consortium. "Appreciative Inquiry is the co-evolutionary, co-operative search for the best in people, their organizations, and the relevant world around them" (Cooperrider, Whitney, & Stavros, 2008, p. 66). This approach is therefore not intended to compare and rank institutions, but is to focus on sharing the lessons learned in each institution, according to their context and highlight the cooperative approach in iKudu. The appreciative enquiry is now in the define stage, focusing on defining the stakeholders related to internationalisation. Details of the results of this piece of research will be reported in a forthcoming publication.

5. Conclusions and next steps

The iKudu project seeks to develop, promote, and embed COIL as a tool for internationalisation at home for all consortium members. By its nature, the project is inclusive as the project strives to ensure students and tutors from across the consortium are able to access and engage in virtual learning through COIL. However, enshrining decolonisation and truly ensuring that all elements of the project are truly equitable remains a key consideration for the project and one that needs careful navigation. Differences in access to technology and class size are examples of inequitable differences that remain and should be addressed in the next phases of the iKudu collaboration.

This paper has shown that COIL can indeed contribute to equality within internationalisation at home activity, by bringing together staff and students of different cultures and working towards a common, global goal. Through its original design and project delivery across Workgroups 1 and 2, iKudu highlights the benefits of COIL in terms of equality.

The main focus for the iKudu consortium now is to continue operating in the ongoing face of the global pandemic in order to realise the crucial work being undertaken across the ten universities. Workgroup 1 will complete its appreciative enquiry in order to share insights into the unique journeys of all consortium members, whilst Workgroup 2 continues to train staff and to assist with the delivery of co-equal, decolonised, Africanised COIL projects. It is perhaps too early to draw conclusions on the impact iKudu will have in South Africa and Europe, but it is clear that it is an important project in terms of capacity building and producing critical research in the field of decolonised education studies.

Finally, iKudu Chair, Cornelius Hagenmeier during an interview conducted on 25th August 2020, noted that the iKudu project's success in managing diversity lies in common goals and shared trust:

> "often, I get asked how we manage to work successfully with such a diverse team. Personally, I think there are two which stand out: the common purpose and the trust capital on which our project has been developed".

It is clear that iKudu's sense of cooperation, trust, and co-equal partnerships will be key to the project having a long-lasting, positive impact.

6. Acknowledgements

The iKudu project is an EU-funded Erasmus+ Capacity Building in HE (CBHE) project (Grant number 610302–EPP-1-2019-1-UK-EPPKA2-CBHE-JP).

References

Agyekum, K. (2018). Linguistic imperialism and language decolonisation in Africa through documentation and preservation. In J. Kandybowicz, T. Major, H. Torrence & P. Duncan (Eds), *African linguistics on the prairie: selected papers from the 45th annual conference on African linguistics*. Language Science Press.

Almeida, J., Robson, S., Morosini, M., & Baranzeli, C. (2019). Understanding Internationalization at home: perspectives from the global north and south. *European Educational Research Journal*, 18(2), 200-217.

Cooperrider, D., Whitney, D., & Stavros, J. (2008). *Appreciative inquiry handbook: for leaders of change*. Berrett-Koehler.

De Wit, H. (2013). Global: Coil—virtual mobility without commercialisation. *Understanding Higher Education Internationalizaiton*, 274, 83-85.

De Wit, H., Hunter F., Howard L., & Egron-Polak E. (2015). (Eds.). *Internationalization of higher education*. European Parliament.

Esche, M. (2018) Incorporating collaborative online international learning (coil) into study abroad courses: a training design. *SIT Digital Collections*. https://core.ac.uk/download/pdf/232740209.pdf

IESA. (2004). *Towards a policy on internationalisation of higher education for South Africa: global, national and institutional imperatives*. International Education Association of South Africa.

Liyange, M. (2020). Miseducation: decolonising curricula, culture and pedagogy in UK universities. *Higher Education Policy Institute*. https://www.hepi.ac.uk/wp-content/uploads/2020/07/HEPI_Miseducation_Debate-Paper-23_FINAL.pdf

Molefe, T.O. (2016). Oppression must fall: South Africa's revolution in theory. *World Policy Journal 33*(1), 30-37. https://doi.org/10.1215/07402775-3545858

Nzimande, E. (2017, April 28). Draft policy framework for the internationalisation of higher education in South Africa. *Government Gazette*.

SUNY COIL. (2020). *Connect, engage, collaborate*. SUNY COIL Center. https://coil.suny.edu/

Van Hove, P. (2019). COIL: what's in an acronym? *EAIE Blog*. https://www.eaie.org/blog/coil-acronym.html

3. The multi-disciplinary approach to an interdisciplinary virtual exchange

Paula Fonseca[1], Kristi Julian[2], Wendi Hulme[3], Maria De Lurdes Martins[4], and Regina Brautlacht[5]

Abstract

New communication technologies are changing the way we work and communicate with people around the world. Given this reality, students in Higher Education (HE) worldwide need to develop knowledge in their area of study as well as attitudes and values that will enable them to be responsible and ethical global citizens in the workforce they will soon enter, regardless of the degree. Different institutional and country-specific requirements are important factors when developing an international Virtual Exchange (VE) program. Digital learning environments such as ProGlobe – Promoting the Global Exchange of Ideas on Sustainable Goals, Practices, and Cultural Diversity – offer a platform for collaborating with diverse students around the world to share and reflect on ideas on sustainable practices. Students work together virtually on a joint interdisciplinary project that aims to create knowledge and foster cultural diversity. This project was successfully integrated into each country's course syllabus through a common global theme; sustainability. The focus of this paper is to present multi-disciplinary perspectives on the opportunities and challenges in implementing a VE project in HE.

1. Polytechnic Institute of Viseu, Viseu, Portugal; paula.fonseca@estgv.ipv.pt; https://orcid.org/0000-0001-8719-0772

2. Middle Tennessee State University, Murfreesboro, Tennessee, United States; kristi.julian@mtsu.edu; https://orcid.org/0000-0002-2512-0549

3. Fanshawe College, London, Ontario, Canada; whulme@fanshawec.ca; https://orcid.org/0000-0002-1700-9410

4. Polytechnic Institute of Viseu, Viseu, Portugal; lurdesmartins@estv.ipv.pt; https://orcid.org/0000-0002-7778-5286

5. Bonn-Rhein-Sieg University of Applied Sciences, Sankt Augustin, Germany; regina.brautlacht@h-brs.de; https://orcid.org/0000-0003-1966-8812

How to cite: Fonseca, P., Julian, K., Hulme, W., Martins, M. D. L., & Brautlacht, R. (2021). The multi-disciplinary approach to an interdisciplinary virtual exchange. In M. Satar (Ed.), *Virtual exchange: towards digital equity in internationalisation* (pp. 41-49). Research-publishing.net. https://doi.org/10.14705/rpnet.2021.53.1288

Furthermore, it will present the challenges that country coordinators dealt with when planning and implementing their project. Given the disparity found in each course syllabus, project coordinators uniquely handled the project goal, approach, and assessment for their specific course and program. Not only did the students and faculty gain valuable insight into different aspects of collaboration when working in interdisciplinary HE projects, they also reflected on their own impact on the environment and learned to listen to how people in different countries deal with environmental issues. This approach provided students with meaningful intercultural experiences that helped them link ideas and concepts about a global issue through the lens of their own discipline as well as other disciplines worldwide.

Keywords: multi-disciplinary approach, interdisciplinary virtual exchange, higher education, sustainability, cultural diversity.

1. Introduction

ProGlobe is a VE project that promotes the global exchange of ideas on sustainable goals, practices, and cultural diversity[6]. It offers a platform for collaborating with diverse students around the world to share and reflect on a global issue. Students from three different disciplines (interior design, tourism, and business) and from four different countries (Canada, Germany, Portugal, and United States) work together virtually on a joint interdisciplinary project that aims to create knowledge and foster cultural diversity. Students in general need to be ready to interact with others in various disciplines. Students in HE worldwide need to develop knowledge in their area of study as well as attitudes and values that will enable them to be responsible and ethical global citizens in the workforce they will soon enter, regardless of the degree (Davies et al., 2018; Denson & Bowman, 2013).

---

6. www.cove.education/proglobe

2. Common link: sustainability

Environmental and economic issues are intrinsically linked. Oftentimes economies are based largely on natural resources, which are not limitless on our planet. In order to maintain these resources, and therefore our economy as well, we must emphasize sustainability. *Our Common Future* (WCED, 1987) was a document put together by the world's leading scientists, research institutions, and government officials whose goal was to politically bring to light environmental issues. It also recognized the interconnectedness of many of the world's concerns and the need for everyone to work together to solve these issues. Based on the premise of providing for 'our common future', the ProGlobe project coordinators determined that focusing the project on a global issue such as sustainability, would ensure easy integration into curriculum for all project partners, and later adaptation for future project partners. Understanding of sustainability requires knowledge of business practices as well as economics. Sustainability provides the bridge and a common thread that could thoughtfully and intentionally be woven into and throughout a variety of curriculum and projects. Knowledge of sustainable products and processes also requires knowledge of the interactions among people and cultures, which was one of the project goals. The scaffolding project provides a platform for students to reflect on resource consumption and sustainability on a global level. The project involves interdisciplinary student teams from across the globe charged with solving a contemporary real-world design problem, which is developed through real-world interviews and presented at a virtual conference each year[7]. Within the context of collaboration, students learn both leadership and teamwork strategies.

3. Project set-up: internationalization and curriculum integration

Once the common link is identified, many factors that vary from country to country are addressed in order to set-up the VE project, such as institutional

---

[7]. cf. https://www.youtube.com/watch?v=fPl_IPYz93M and https://youtu.be/SxHAnE2az4I

Chapter 3

and country requirements, technology, and scheduling. In the ProGlobe project, strict adherence to policies for data protection and research ethics are followed early in the set-up of the project as part of the institutional and country requirements. For example, in North America, required compliance with the Research Ethics Board mandates that students provide signed informed consent once they are apprised of the research objective to protect all participants, and the dissemination requirements of the research results to eliminate identifiable information (Conestoga, 2011).

Another critical component in setting up a VE project is technology, as appropriate equipment and training for both faculty and students must be acquired prior to the start of the project, and access to technology varies from country to country. In addition, ongoing maintenance of the project materials, submissions, and digital platform must be scheduled from the beginning of the project, through to the end. To address the technological and scheduling challenges, coordinators as well as their students use synchronous collaborative tools (Zoom and/or Skype) as well as asynchronous tools, such as emails, Google Docs, and Google Spreadsheets. Coordinators also share information on Slack, an online messaging platform.

Which course will the VE be integrated into? The program or course selection depends, not only on the course topic, but on the program outcomes and course outcomes. The VE project should enrich the learning experience toward the intended student outcomes in the course (Rutherford, 2014).

How will the VE be integrated into the program or course? The level of integration of the VE into the program or course must be determined by assessing whether the VE will be an entire course, a project over several weeks, or a one-time experiential task that will ensure the most effective alignment with the program and course outcomes.

What credit will be awarded for the VE? What will the grade weight be for the VE toward the final course grade? The length and complexity of the VE will affect this determination, as will the effectiveness of the VE to meet the program and course outcomes.

4. ProGlobe: a multi-disciplinary approach

However, a new level of complexity is introduced into this consideration of curriculum integration when the VE project includes multiple disciplines, beyond the complexity of multiple institutions in multiple countries. In the ProGlobe VE project, we address this by introducing the unique integration of the VE into each course, program, and/or institution; a *multi-disciplinary approach*. It is determined that flexibility must be provided to each country coordinator (faculty) in order to most effectively align the project with each of the varied discipline foci separately. ProGlobe is a six-week project that is integrated into an existing course, which accommodates this flexibility. To maintain the quality, consistency, and relevance of the ProGlobe project, a balance of fixed versus flexible project components is established. The flexible components include:

- unique alignment of the VE project and goals with the course at each institution;

- unique assignment of the grade weight for the VE project within the total course grade at each institution; and

- unique integration of the course-specific discipline as a focus for the final student presentations at each institution.

The flexibility of these components simplifies the integration of the VE project in order to promote this mode of global and culturally diverse experience for students. The fixed components of the ProGlobe project are contained within a shared student guidelines document to ensure consistency in project instruction, tasks, and student submissions throughout the program by all faculty and all students in all countries. The student guidelines document provides a project plan and schedule (see Table 1), itemized task instruction, and supporting resources and templates for all required student submissions. While the project sequence, instruction, and tasks are consistent, the tasks are broadly focused, which allows students from multiple disciplines to easily adjust their focus for their final submission more specifically to their own discipline.

Chapter 3

Table 1. ProGlobe 2019 project management plan: the stages and tasks

Phases	Dates	Task overview	
I	September 30 – October 06	Orientation	Welcome Message and Project Orientation from Coordinators in Canada, Germany, Portugal, and the USA
	October 07 – October 13	Task A: Footprint Analysis	Information on Sustainable Footprints, join one of the five research teams and get acquainted with the field of research
	October 14 – October 20	Task B: Personal Log	Collect personal data about your footprint behavior
	October 21 – October 27	Task C: Cultural Interviews	Conduct an informal interview about a cultural topic
	October 28 – November 03	Task D: Research Interviews	Conduct and record a research interview as well as be interviewed by another student from abroad
II	November 4 – November 10	Task E: Presentation	Prepare a presentation on research topic and cultural interviews, demonstrating learning outcomes
III	November 12	Task F: Virtual Conference	Organize, conduct, and attend a virtual conference
IV	November 18 – November 22	Task G: Documentation and Project Evaluation	Reflect on the research assignments, compile all documents from your country, and complete the online evaluation of the project

This table exemplifies a project management plan that was put into practice in the 2019 ProGlobe project. It shows an overview of the different phases, tasks, and deadlines in this specific project. Please note that some phases run parallel. Each phase has a particular deadline when the task is to be completed and uploaded on the project wiki.

5. Implementation of multi-disciplinary approach into ProGlobe

The implementation of *the multi-disciplinary approach* into the ProGlobe project begins with the review of each program and course for opportunities of curriculum integration. A review of the program/degree outcomes, course outcomes, and accreditation outcomes in all four institutions of the ProGlobe project reveal common outcome foci in various areas, specifically in cultural diversity and sustainability. For example, for Portugal, the tourism program strives to connect innovation and evolution of tourism with other sectors within a sustainable network. Their course outcomes revolve around social, cultural, and linguistic awareness in sustainable tourism practices. For the United States and Canada, the accreditation requirements are the same and focus on cultural diversity within a global, societal, economic, and environmental context as well as sustainable design, cultural sensitivity, and multicultural influences. For Germany and the business program, the goal is to introduce students to concepts of sustainable business practices. As a result of this review, the ProGlobe project is integrated into the course from each institution where these outcomes best align with the goals of the project.

Given the specificities of each course, each country coordinator decides how they will embed the project into their course syllabus and who will participate. In Canada and the US, the ProGlobe project is introduced mid-semester as a component of a larger design project within the discipline and, therefore, all the students (20) participate. The same holds true for Germany, where all the students (20) also participate. The ProGlobe project for this specific country is the initial project of a larger English communications project. The tourism degree in Portugal; however, implements the project differently from the other three partner countries. The ProGlobe project is a voluntary-based standalone project that students can choose to do for course credit instead of another tourism related project. In 2019, despite the high enrollment rate of that academic year (+/- 40 students), only 30% agreed to take part due to many different factors. Personal motivation was the main factor. Those who chose the ProGlobe project in 2019 as their semester project, did so because sustainability was a topic that highly interested them, while others were more motivated toward other topics.

To ensure and maintain project motivation and commitment throughout the project, it is fundamental that each country coordinator decides the grade weight of the VE project within the final course grade. This decision is closely related to whether the project is considered a standalone project or a component of a larger project during the semester. It is not surprising that Portugal attributes the highest percentage rate (60%) of its total course assessment to the project given that ProGlobe is a standalone project within the course. The other three countries weighted the project with similar percentages (USA: 25%; Canada: 20%, and Germany: 20%) within their final course assessment given that the VE project is a component of a larger project.

6. Project results and conclusion

To conclude, students in HE need to develop global competencies such as cross-cultural collaborations, and learn how to work on multi-disciplinary teams to build on 21st century skills in order to be competent professionals when they enter the workforce. Multi-disciplinary VE projects like ProGlobe encourage these students to do just that. This VE allows students to learn aspects of teamwork, teambuilding, and project management within an international scope. The nature of the structure and scaffolding in the project aids in project tasks and is clearly seen in student learning outcomes.

This project also provides students with an environmental and social global awareness at a personal level by allowing students to evaluate and reflect on their own sustainable practices as well as at a global level by interviewing students from other disciplines and countries to share and discuss these reflections and understand the issues from different cultural perspectives.

Finally, students gain the ability to link ideas and concepts through the lens of different disciplines through an intercultural experience, which is witnessed in the virtual conference at the end of the project. It is in this conference that students from all countries are able to present common sustainable topics with a focus on their own discipline, while also gaining a multi-discipline perspective by listening to other students from other countries presenting their discipline-focused findings.

References

Conestoga. (2011, June 16). *G_9: Ethical conduct in research involving humans in research*. Conestoga College Institute of Technology and Advanced Learning. https://cms.conestogac.on.ca/sites/corporate-websites/policies/PDFDocuments/Applied%20Research/Ethical%20Conduct%20in%20Research%20Involving%20Humans.pdf

Davies, I., Ho, L., Kiwan, D., Peck, C.L., Peterson, A., Sant, E., & Waghid, Y. (2018). *The Palgrave handbook of global citizenship and education*. Springer. https://doi.org/10.1057/978-1-137-59733-5

Denson, N., & Bowman, N. (2013). University diversity and preparation for a global society: the role of diversity in shaping intergroup attitudes and civic outcomes. *Studies in Higher Education, 38*(4), 555-570. https://doi.org/10.1080/03075079.2011.584971

Rutherford, S. (2014). *Collaborative learning: theory, strategies, and educational benefits*. Nova Science Publishers, Inc.

WCED. (1987). *Our common future: the world commission on environment and development*. Oxford University Press.

4. Creating a prototype for a seawater farm through an American-Tunisian virtual exchange

Nadia Cheikhrouhou[1] and Kenneth Ludwig[2]

Abstract

This paper will discuss a Virtual Exchange (VE) between the University of Michigan (USA) and the High Institute of Technological Studies of Béja (Tunisia) that took place between October and December 2019. Students from Tunisia and USA were enrolled in two entrepreneurship courses in their respective universities and joined together to work in groups on an innovative project on 'creating a prototype for a seawater farm in the region of Khniss' to be presented at the end of the semester. As this project was student-centered, the main focus was to show its impact on the students through their testimonials on what challenges they encountered and what benefits they gained from this experience at an academic and personal level. These testimonials showed that despite differences in intercultural communication competencies between American and Tunisian students and the use of English as a lingua franca, students gained valuable skills in team communication, collaboration, and coordination in a large team spread over two continents. Students taught each other and learned from each other while working toward solving a social and environmental problem the world is struggling with. Another light was shed on the impact of this VE on the instructors, the pedagogy adopted to conduct the project, as well as the contribution of the instructional support staff.

1. High Institute of Technological Studies of Béja, Béja, Tunisia; nadiachikhrouhou@yahoo.com; https://orcid.org/0000-0003-4849-3134

2. University of Michigan, Ann Arbor, USA; ken.ludwig@gmail.com; https://orcid.org/0000-0003-3186-3645

How to cite: Cheikhrouhou, N., & Ludwig, K. (2021). Creating a prototype for a seawater farm through an American-Tunisian virtual exchange. In M. Satar (Ed.), *Virtual exchange: towards digital equity in internationalisation* (pp. 51-60). Research-publishing.net. https://doi.org/10.14705/rpnet.2021.53.1289

Chapter 4

Moving from a directive to a student-driven approach was rewarding for the Tunisian instructor who learned how to push students out of their comfort zone, dive into uncertain areas, and ask questions rather than accepting the norms. On his part the American instructor learned that it is possible to create meaningful, unconventional student-led projects across languages, cultures, and geography as long as the teams (students and faculty) are excited and committed to the project. He also learned that students get inspired to be brave, thoughtful, and resourceful when they can witness what effective professional collaboration by faculty looks like.

Keywords: seawater farm, problem-based learning, virtual collaboration.

1. Introduction

Water scarcity is a huge challenge in Tunisia. In fact, due to its arid to semi-arid climate, "Tunisia [is] facing increasingly […] serious water shortage problems, [it is therefore important] to develop additional water resources as well as to preserve the existing ones" (Bahri, 2002, p. 2). Moreover, climate change is likely to place further pressure on water resources (Obeng, Bahri, & Grobik, 2015). This challenging situation was at the heart of a VE between students from the USA and Tunisia who worked on developing a prototype for a seawater farm instead of tackling the water scarcity problem. Students were split into five teams, each focusing on a different aspect on developing a successful seawater farm: legal, social, and cultural aspect, engineering aspect, environmental aspect, financial aspect, and finally marketing and communication aspect. Students were encouraged in this project to find an inexpensive solution based on existing scarce resources and the prototype was a farming sustainable system plan that exploited natural local resources in the region of Khniss in Tunisia. The instructional method adopted was a problem-based learning approach based on four current insights into learning: constructive, self-directed, collaborative, and contextual (Dolmans, De Grave, Wolfhagen, & Van Der Vleuten, 2005). This approach frames a space "for students to learn to [be] active agents, creators of change during their university studies and [...] continue to be habitual agents and creators when they leave university to live and work in an uncertain, [complex] world" (Kek & Huijser, 2015, p. 410). Through this approach students are more likely to develop the right "skills to take risks, to reason critically, to reflect, to be resourceful, and to be autonomous – qualities of lifelong learners – which will allow them to work and live productively in a world of uncertainties" (Kek & Huijser, 2015, p. 408).

The aim of the current paper is to report on this VE: its context, its results and challenges, its impact on students, and finally the role of the instructors and the instructional support staff.

2. The context of the VE

This VE was conducted between October and December 2019 between the High Institute of Technological Studies of Béja and the University of Michigan. Thirty-five students participated in this VE, 25 from Michigan enrolled in ALA 256: The Innovator's Toolkit course and ten from Béja enrolled in the Entrepreneurship course. Students were asked to create a blueprint for a sea water farm that would be built in a real-world location, in this case, Khniss, Tunisia.

Khniss is a small city located on the eastern coast of Tunisia. It features a marine depression with two levels in the sea; the first level is a confined lagoon with no significant marine waves or currents called by the locals the 'Dead Sea', and a second level with moderate waves and currents called the 'Live Sea'. The lagoon used to have a particularly rich marine biodiversity which has been endangered in the last few decades by pollution due to urban and industrial waste. In addition, the water shortage is becoming an increasing problem especially during the dry season because water resources are diverted to the tourism sector.

To create a blueprint for a seawater farm in Khniss, students were split into five teams. Each team had its own goal (Table 1).

Table 1. Goals of the different teams

Team	Goal
Agriculture and environment	Use the salty Mediterranean water to farm crops that could feed a community of 5,000 people in a sustainable way with little to no negative environmental side effects
Engineering	Create infrastructure that produces food, water, and energy for 5,000 people
Finance	Make the project financially feasible and sustainable
Law, location, culture	Make sure that the project respects the laws and the culture of the area
Marketing communication and strategy	Promote the project to the world

Each team was composed of five American and two Tunisian students from different disciplines (computer sciences, mechanical engineering, psychology etc.) and from different levels of studies. This multidisciplinarity helped enrich the exchange of ideas and co-construction of knowledge (McLean, 2009).

To achieve their goals, teams made a lot of research and talked to experts in the field from both countries. In addition, four students from Béja traveled to Khniss and interviewed locals to understand their needs and their problems, and to collect their opinions and suggestions about the project.

The outcome was a seawater farm plan that is inexpensive, eco-friendly with a low carbon footprint, and sustainable using local natural resources and respecting local diet and culture. First seawater is channeled from the sea to fish farms, then the water from these farms is channeled into farms that grow Salicornia and Mangroves which are trees that can remove salt from the water and make it suitable for human consumption and agricultural use. Students worked synchronously via WhatsApp and Messenger and asynchronously on Google Docs. Each team also created a YouTube video and a website[3], for the whole project was created using Wix to share its outcomes with the world.

---

3. https://rgmartin25.wixsite.com/seawaterfarm/what-we-do

Students from Béja and Michigan presented their final project together virtually using the Blue Jeans videoconferencing tool. All the technical aspects of this videoconference were managed by the instructional support staff of the University of Michigan. At the end of the VE, students were also asked to reflect on their experience.

3. Results and challenges

Students from both Béja and Michigan made written reflections at the end of the project on their telecollaboration using the 'What? So What? Now What?' reflective model (Rolfe, Freshwater, & Jasper, 2001). Below are some of the testimonies of participants' experiences of their telecollaboration with colleagues from the other institution, in another country.

One participant from the University of Michigan highlighted the friendship formed and the cultural exchange that occurred:

> "this experience was great because it allowed me to work with others around the world and learn from them things that I would otherwise not have learned. It has also allowed me to learn more about another country and its culture which is very important to better help reduce the discrimination in the world. Last but not least I made a friend all the way across the world".

Another participant from the USA talked about the importance of multidisciplinarity in the team:

> "I personally believe that our team's connection with [Name of a student from Tunisia] was the most important part of our project. I learned that we should be willing to learn from one another, especially because our peers have expertise in various areas, and we can learn a lot from their experiences and knowledge set. As a current student of physical therapy, I now focus my studying methods on learning from my

> classmates. Especially during COVID-times, Zoom study groups have been an extremely useful study tool for me. It truly amazes me how another person's perspective can show you various paths in approaching a problem".

So this VE helped students to explore new perspectives and see the world from a different lens. They discovered new cultures and new ways of collaboration across geography. They felt like they were complementing each other to achieve a noble cause. One participant from Tunisia added:

> "on the 10th of November 2019 I found myself on a road trip to discover my own country going to Khniss for the first time ever, I didn't even know that this place existed before the project".

By interviewing locals in Khniss, students developed their empathy skills. By trying to understand and solve the water issue in the region of Khniss, students enhanced their community engagement and global citizenship competencies. Talking about challenges in online collaboration one participant from the University of Michigan commented:

> "as you might imagine, keeping everyone on the same page was challenging, and we had to adapt quickly in order to ensure everyone remained on the same page. We did this through regularly communicating with the other teams".

As mentioned in the last testimonial, communication within the groups was sometimes challenging due mainly to the difference in intercultural communicative competence between American and Tunisian students on the one hand and the use of English as the language of instruction on the other hand. As a matter of fact, compared to Tunisian students, American peers live in a more culturally diverse society. This could probably create an imbalance in terms of intercultural communicative competence in favor of American students who were more flexible than their Tunisian counterparts who additionally have no mobility opportunities and had no previous international experience.

Moreover there were also some issues related to the language of the exchange, i.e. English as a lingua franca. In Tunisia, English as a foreign language negatively impacted some students' ability to communicate with their American partners who dominated the group. That is why in each group the Tunisian instructor made sure that there is at least one Tunisian student who is fluent in English to communicate directly with American peers.

4. The role of the instructors

Before the VE, both instructors had different pedagogical approaches. Indeed, the American instructor was creating a much more ambiguous and complex environment of learning for his students than the Tunisian one by providing little guidance for a complex project.

As one of the American students stated:

> "at first, when we were introduced to this project, I was very confused. No one knew what a seawater farm was and there is little on the internet explaining this concept. All we had to go off of was a quick doodle our instructor drew in an attempt to make the vision more clear. However this did not help. One thing that did however help was when our instructor told us that 'now is not the time to have answers just try to ask as many questions as possible', this allowed me to take the pressure off of myself and realize that I can work at my own pace as long as I accomplish what I need to get done. This allowed me to quickly adjust and strive during the project".

And since entrepreneurs act in a VUCA (Volatile, Uncertain, Complex, and Ambiguous) world, or what Barnett calls the age of supercomplexity "in which there are no stable descriptions of the world, no concepts that can be seized upon with any assuredness, and no value systems that can claim one's allegiance with any unrivaled authority" (Barnett, 2004, p. 252), it is important to simulate this environment for students in the entrepreneurship class.

So, the role of the instructors was not to lecture but to listen very attentively to what students were saying and the learning that was taking place in the team, and to ask questions that encouraged critical thinking and encouraging students to be responsible to complete high quality independent learning (Barrett & Cashman, 2010, p. 11). In this VE, instructors decided that it was better to say less – or even nothing – and to provide students with minimal guidance so they could feel that they were taking the lead in the learning by asking the right questions and researching for possible answers. This was new for the Tunisian instructor – who before this VE had adopted a more directive pedagogy – which brought her out of her safe zone but she was eager to challenge herself and learn new things. What she learned from her American partner was to push students to be uncomfortable – most students had never even heard of a seawater farm before – dive into uncertain areas, and ask questions rather than accept the standards. This was challenging at first for the Tunisian students who were used to strict rules and regulations set in place by their professors but the collaborative work they had with their American partners helped them take ownership over their learning: they were doing research, talking about their findings, teaching each other, and learning from each other.

The American instructor learned that it is possible to create unconventional student led projects across languages, cultures, and geography. He believed that bold vision gets further pedagogically and leads to greater impact than tightly scripted and controlled faculty driven efforts and that trusted colleagues provide the bridges over the chasms that may appear.

Another question discussed between the instructors was whether to have groups competing against each other or collaborating. The collaborative option was preferred with interrelated groups and the success of the whole project depending on the efforts and the commitment of each group. This added on one hand more complexity to the problem to be solved and on the other hand allowed for the opportunity for each group to reflect on its contribution and how much this contribution was important for the other groups and for the success of the whole project.

Also, it is important to mention that the participation of the instructional support staff of the University of Michigan was very important for the success of this project since they were constantly communicating with both the instructors and the students to provide help when necessary and coordinating the whole process. They ensured all the logistical parts of the VE, like organizing different Zoom meetings with the two instructors to monitor the project. They also organized the videoconference for the final presentations of the different teams and tested in that regard the Blue Jeans tool with the students from Béja. They were seen by all as full, essential, and equal partners in the project.

5. Conclusion

This VE aimed to contribute to the development of "key transferable skills for work and social life of the students: Critical thinking skills, Problem solving skills, Research skills, Creative thinking skills, Communication skills, Teamwork skills [and] Information literacy skills" (Barrett & Cashman, 2010, p. 10). It showed that it is possible to create meaningful student led projects across languages, culture, and geography. Students realized a seawater farm plan that is cost effective and sustainable using natural local resources and respecting the natural ecosystem in the region of Khniss. This required them to be empathetic, creative, and flexible to adapt to the local context of Khniss which are key competencies for entrepreneurs.

Both instructors learned from each other as well and felt growing at a personal and professional level through this VE. Their role was mainly to make sure that the learning environment allows students to deal with uncertainty in productive and creative ways. They saw their function to be facilitators of the whole process by monitoring if necessary, improving the quality of the discussion in the group, and allocating the responsibility of learning on learners. They also had the responsibility to ensure a collaborative learning environment where students share common goals, and are dependent on and accountable to each other.

Finally we can add that in the interconnected world we are living in it is important that students think across borders to solve global issues.

6. Acknowledgments

The authors are grateful to Philomena Meechan and Todd Austin, the instructional support staff of the University of Michigan, Allison Westra and Isabella Przybylska, teaching assistants at the University of Michigan, and the students: Lorenzo Harris, Iheb Merai, Bahaeddine Chouchène, and Rahee Patel.

References

Bahri, A. (2002). Water reuse in Tunisia: state and prospective. *Actes de l'atelier du PCSI, Montpellier, France, 28-29 May 2002.*

Barnett, R. (2004). Learning in an unknown future. *Higher Education Research and Development, 23*(3), 247-260. https://doi.org/10.1080/0729436042000235382

Barrett, T., & Cashman, D. (2010). (Eds). *A practitioner's guide to enquiry and problem-based learning: case studies from University College Dublin.* UCD Teaching and Learning. https://dokumen.tips/documents/constructivism-problem-based-learning.html

Dolmans, D. H., De Grave, W., Wolfhagen, I. H., & Van Der Vleuten, C. P. (2005). Problem-based learning: future challenges for educational practice and research. *Med Educ, 39*(7), 732-741. https://doi.org/10.1111/j.1365-2929.2005.02205.x

Kek, M., & Huijser, H. (2015). 21st century skills: problem-based learning and the University of the Future. *Proceedings of the Third 21st Century Academic Forum Conference, Harvard, Boston, USA, 20-22 September 2015.*

McLean, M. (2009). Critical mass. In P. Ramsden (Ed.), *Teachers as learners – the development of academic staff* (pp. 24-26). HEA: Academy Exchange.

Obeng, A., Bahri, A., & Grobik, A. (2015). Water scarcity and global megacities. In J. Osikena & D. Tickner (Eds), *Tackling the world water crisis: reshaping the future of foreign policy.* Policy Center.

Rolfe, G., Freshwater, D., & Jasper, M. (2001). *Critical reflection in nursing and the helping professions: a user's guide.* Palgrave Macmillan.

Section 2.
Digital communication skills

5. Compensatory strategies adopted by Chinese EFL learners in virtual exchange with native speakers

Ruiling Feng[1] and Sheida Shirvani[2]

Abstract

Compensatory strategies play an important role in second language (L2) processing because of limited language knowledge and ensuing anxiety and could help assure understanding and void communication breakdown. Previous studies about compensatory strategies largely adopt laboratory settings and neglect the strategies in authentic oral communication. Accordingly, the present study investigated compensatory strategies used by Chinese university students in online videoconferences with their US peers during a five-week virtual exchange project. We interviewed 27 Chinese students twice, once after the first-week videoconference, the other after the last-week videoconference. The English as a Foreign Language (EFL) learners in this study could adopt compensatory strategies of different levels. Their strategy use, however, was not flexible enough as several types of strategies were repeatedly used, while other types were rarely implemented. The virtual exchange could help the EFL learners employ compensatory strategies more often, of higher levels, and with increased immediacy. The results can help to establish more targeted English teaching and learning.

Keywords: compensatory strategy, virtual exchange, videoconference, English as a foreign language, China's standards of English language ability.

---

1. Tianjin Normal University, Tianjin, China; fengruiling@126.com; https://orcid.org/0000-0002-2482-3146

2. Ohio University, Zanesville, United States; shirvani@ohio.edu; https://orcid.org/0000-0002-7537-7318

How to cite: Feng, R., & Shirvani, S. (2021). Compensatory strategies adopted by Chinese EFL learners in virtual exchange with native speakers. In M. Satar (Ed.), *Virtual exchange: towards digital equity in internationalisation* (pp. 63-71). Research-publishing.net. https://doi.org/10.14705/rpnet.2021.53.1290

Chapter 5

1. Literature review

L2 processing features a high frequency of compensation because of limited language knowledge and ensuing language anxiety (Cieslicka & Heredia, 2011; Galloway, 1981, 1982; Paradis, 1998). English learners often encounter difficulties in initiating and maintaining conversations (Hyter, 2017; Wolfson, 1989), and communication breakdowns result from an inadequate active vocabulary (Poulisse, 1987). These difficulties may hamper collaborative learning with peers. Research has shown that bilinguals exhibit a higher pragmatic sensitivity than monolinguals (Groba et al., 2017) and rely more on pragmatic and paralinguistic cues to achieve understanding and successive output (Yow & Markman, 2011). Those with low L2 proficiency evoke greater adoption of compensatory strategies. Paribakht (1985) mentioned that communication strategy use and proficiency level were related. Poulisse (1987) posited that foreign language proficiency mainly affected the number of compensatory strategies. Poulisse and Schils (2006) later found that proficiency levels were inversely related to the number of compensatory strategies.

Previous studies about compensatory strategies largely adopt an experimental approach that neglects authentic oral communication. Accordingly, this study proposed a descriptive study on compensatory strategies by learners of EFL in natural communication via videoconferences with native English speakers over a five-week virtual exchange project. This study aimed to investigate how Chinese EFL learners used compensatory strategies in a virtual exchange with US native English speakers and how the exchange changed EFL learners' strategy use.

2. Methods

2.1. Context and participants

A total of 27 participants at a university in China participated in the study. They were all Mandarin native speakers, second-year university EFL learners. They participated in a five-week virtual exchange project between an English-skill-based course at their university and a cultural communication course at a US university. During the project, the Chinese EFL learners and 20 US students (all native English speakers) were grouped into ten international groups, each with two to three EFL learners and two native speakers. Every week, each international group held a videoconference on Zoom (free version) in which students interviewed and were interviewed by their international partners following a semi-structured interview approach focusing on a particular topic each week. Each videoconference lasted for at least 30 minutes, with no upper limit.

2.2. Data collection and analysis

We collected data from students' weekly Zoom meeting recordings and interviews. Students were required to submit the recordings as a weekly assignment for the instructors to monitor the progress of their exchange. Eight groups managed to submit all their five meeting recordings, while the other two groups did not, and therefore we abandoned their recordings in data analysis. We carefully watched and coded the total 40 recordings with when and what compensatory strategies were used. All the EFL learners gave us their consent to analyze for academic purposes their English production in the virtual exchange.

Two semi-structured interviews were conducted with each Chinese student, after the first and the last videoconferences following a similar protocol. Typical questions included *Did you use XX strategy often in the Zoom meeting, why and why not?*, *What have you learned concerning dealing with expression difficulty in speaking English?*, and *What will you do if you meet XX difficulties in the Zoom meeting?*. The coding of meeting recordings and interview protocol was developed based on the table *Oral expression strategies: assessment and compensation* in China's Standards of English language ability (CSE[3], p. 69). The CSE classifies different compensatory strategies into nine levels. Each level contains several types of strategies. Given that most EFL learners' English

---

3. http://cse.neea.edu.cn/html1/report/18112/9627-1.htm

level in this study falls between CSE Levels 4 to 7 (based on the instructor's evaluation), the present study only included types of compensatory strategies of Levels 4 to 7. The participants' English proficiency was assessed according to their scores in College English Test – Band 4 (CET-4), a test of English proficiency widely recognized in Mainland China (Guo & Sun, 2014). The interviews were conducted in Chinese for more precise understanding and more accurate responses. Then the interview recordings were transcribed and analyzed by thematic data analysis methods. First, we grouped repeating ideas from related passages, synthesized themes by organizing repeating ideas into coherent categories, developed theoretical constructs by grouping themes into more abstract concepts, and finally discussed the results based on related theories and previous studies. We also compared the first-round interview data with the second-round interview data.

3. Results and discussion

3.1. Every EFL learner could adopt compensatory strategies of different levels

Through meeting recordings and interviews, we tried to classify EFL learners' compensation competence into different levels. However, it was not feasible as students' compensatory skills were not consistent. For example, one student could infer meaning from context or paralinguistic features (CSE Level 7), but she could not appropriately use paralinguistic features such as stress (CSE Level 5), or self-correction (CSE Level 6).

Also, the compensatory strategies used by the Chinese EFL learners were unevenly distributed within each level. Some strategies were widely adopted; others of the same level, however, were seldom used. For example, many students often inferred meaning from context (CSE Level 7), but very few students tried to confirm details by asking further questions or interject in others' talk for clarification (CSE Level 7). The lack of confirmation and clarification might be caused by the fear that the EFL learners think: "clarification request is face-threatening especially in an intercultural context". According to the interview data, the uneven distribution was more related to students' conversational styles than to English proficiency.

3.2. Videoconference-based virtual exchange could help EFL learners better apply compensatory strategies

Overall, the EFL learners in this study made progress in trying compensatory strategies more often, of higher levels, and with increased immediacy. Most interviewees reported that they could gradually conduct more timely and dynamic assessments of their oral expressions, and noticed and corrected more language errors with a shorter delay. When misunderstanding occurred in the later phase of the virtual exchange, they gradually tried to request clarification and elaboration from their international partners.

Students owed the development of compensatory strategies concerning the frequency, level, and immediacy to the increased ease and confidence in and courage of speaking English online with their US peers. Familiarity with virtual co-presence, intercultural communication, and their international peers promoted those positive emotions, according to the second-round interview. As one interviewee mentioned,

> "at the beginning of the project, I had to rehearse what I wanted to say and then join the discussion, and also, I felt super anxious if I cannot understand my US partners, but later I found they could understand me despite my grammatical mistakes, so I gradually relaxed and plucked my courage to talk more, to confirm or ask for clarification. They are always very nice and patient to explain".

Therefore, the development of their compensatory strategies was related to a more optimized use of English, positive feelings (such as confidence and courage), improved digital literacy (increasing familiarity with Zoom-based videoconferences), and increased proximity with the virtual exchange partners.

3.3. English proficiency affected EFL learners' choice of compensatory strategies

The Chinese students with higher English proficiency were more flexible with different compensatory strategies, compensated in a timelier manner for an error or a gap between what they wanted to say and what they could say, adopted more compensatory strategies of higher level, and helped their Chinese peers compensate with communication breakdowns. This finding corroborated previous studies (Paribakht, 1985; Poulisse, 1987). In interviews, one student said: "when I noticed my local partners were silent for quite a moment, I would 'cue' them with questions, so they could join the conversation". In Zoom recordings, we observed that lower-proficiency students, on the contrary, compensated less, used fewer types of strategies and fewer high-level strategies, and showed longer delay before the compensation, as they had a bigger gap between 'what they want to say' and 'what they can say'. One student said in the interview: "I felt frustrated sometimes because when I figured out how to express my idea, the moment had already gone".

It seems that English proficiency influenced the attentional resource EFL learners invested in meaning transfer and focus on language form or logical flow. Students with higher English levels were more likely to have additional attentional resources to notice their non-target-like language use, incomplete understanding, and illogical flow, and therefore, they were more cognitively capable of compensation behaviors.

3.4. Chinese EFL learners tended to avoid clarification requests, confirmation checks, and comprehension checks

Chinese EFL learners tended to avoid asking further questions to the interlocutor (clarification request or confirmation check) and checking understandings (comprehension check) despite frequent comprehension difficulty and non-understanding among their partners. They would rather search online or ask people physically around them or their Chinese partners on WeChat, as they reckoned that it was less face-threatening than asking for clarification or confirmation in the Zoom meeting room with the presence of their US partners. "I don't want them [US students] to think that I'm incapable of communicating in English, so I would rather figure things out by myself or ask my Chinese partners later", one interviewee said. They left comprehension checks to the listeners, assuming that the local and international partners would ask for clarification if necessary.

When being asked about reasons why they did not take initiatives to confirm comprehension or clarify confusion, they generally mentioned that "I don't think it's polite to interject while that person was still talking", "since our US partners are native speakers, I would assume it's because my English isn't good enough to understand them", "it's easier to ask my Chinese partners or search online first". Also, the Chinese students were so cognitively occupied with producing English spontaneously in a virtually co-present environment that they did not have the extra cognitive resources to confirm their interlocutors' understanding. Another common reason was that the Chinese students assumed these behaviors suggested incapability or lack of confidence in themselves or their interlocutors.

3.5. EFL meaning above form

Most interviewees said that they were more focused on communication than on correction so self-repair was mainly done only when the errors affected the message and interaction. The process of self-initiated repair encompasses questioning the meaning or correctness of a language form produced by oneself, noticing errors, and correcting them subsequently (Leeser, 2004).

To self-repair an error, the EFL learners have to allocate selective attention to the gap between their interlanguage and target language (Gass & Torres, 2005) and take initiative to fill up the gap. The self-initiated repair was rare for the errors with low communicative load because the communication in this study was generally meaning-oriented and featured high immediacy, and most of the time interlocutors would not focus on language forms as such behavior might impact the communication flow.

4. Conclusions

This study has shown that virtual exchanges could boost students' compensatory strategies use, improving their communicative skills. In addition, the five-week videoconference recordings and pre/post interview data gathered in the interviews showed that practice and getting to know the interlocutors increased confidence and improved the use of EFL. Thus, the participation of EFL learners in virtual exchanges on a regular basis could make a difference in their EFL skills. In this sense, virtual exchange offers a meaningful and less costly natural communication environment compared with international physical mobility. We also argue that future virtual exchanges with a longer duration can be more helpful in improving communication skills.

5. Acknowledgments

This study was supported by the Tianjin philosophy and social science project 'International collaboration community of tertiary-level English teaching-learning-research in 'Internet +' era' (TJWW16-018) and the Project of Discipline Innovation and Advancement (PODIA)-Foreign Language Education Studies at Beijing Foreign Studies University (Grant Number: 2020SYLZDXM011), Beijing.

References

Cieslicka, A. B., & Heredia, R. R. (2011). Hemispheric asymmetries in processing L1 and L2 idioms: effects of salience and context. *Brain & Language, 116*(3), 136-150. https://doi.org/10.1016/j.bandl.2010.09.007

Galloway, L. M. (1981). *Contributions of the right cerebral hemisphere to language and communication: issues in cerebral dominance with special emphasis on bilingualism, second language acquisition, sex differences and certain ethnic groups*. Ph.D. dissertation. Department of Linguistics. University of California at Los Angeles.

Galloway, L. M. (1982). Bilingualism: neuropsychological considerations. *Journal of Research & Development in Education, 15*, 12-28.

Gass, S., & Torres, M. J. (2005). Attention when?: an investigation of the ordering effect of input and interaction. *Studies in Second Language Acquisition, 27*(1), 1-31.

Groba, A., De Houwer, A., Mehnert, J., Rossi, S., & Obrig, H. (2017). Bilingual and monolingual children process pragmatic cues differently when learning novel adjectives. *Bilingualism: Language and Cognition*, 1-19. https://doi.org/10.1017/S1366728917000232

Guo, Q., & Sun, W. (2014). Economic returns to English proficiency for college graduates in Mainland China. *China Economic Review, 30*, 290-300. https://doi.org/10.1016/j.chieco.2014.07.014

Hyter, Y. D. (2017). Pragmatic assessment and intervention in children. In L. Cummings (Ed.), *Research in clinical pragmatics, perspectives in pragmatics, philosophy & psychology* (pp. 493-526). Springer International Publishing. https://doi.org/10.1007/978-3-319-47489-2_19

Leeser, M. J. (2004). Learner proficiency and focus on form during collaborative dialogue. *Language Teaching Research, 8*(1), 55-81. https://doi.org/10.1191/1362168804lr134oa

Paradis, M. (1998). language and communication in multilinguals. In B. Stemmer & W. A. Whitaker (Eds), *Handbook of neurolinguistics* (pp. 417-430). Academic Press. https://doi.org/10.1016/b978-012666055-5/50033-2

Paribakht, T. (1985). Strategic competence and language proficiency. *Applied Linguistics, 6*, 132-146. https://doi.org/10.1093/applin/6.2.132

Poulisse, N. (1987). Problems and solutions in the classification of compensatory strategies. *Second Language Research, 3*(2), 141-153.

Poulisse, N., & Schils, E. (2006). The influence of task and proficiency-related factors on the use of compensatory strategies: a quantitative analysis. *Language Learning, 39*(1), 15-46. https://doi.org/10.1111/j.1467-1770.1989.tb00590.x

Wolfson, N. (1989). The social dynamics of native and nonnative variation in complimenting behavior. In M. Eisenstein (Ed.), *The dynamic interlanguage: empirical studies in second language acquisition* (pp. 219-236). Plenum. https://doi.org/10.1007/978-1-4899-0900-8_14

Yow, W. Q., & Markman, E. M. (2011). Bilingualism and children's use of paralinguistic cues to interpret emotion in speech. *Bilingualism: Language and Cognition, 14*(4), 562-569. https://doi.org/10.1017/s1366728910000404

6. Supporting intercultural communication with visual information in virtual exchanges: when a picture paints a thousand words

Marta Fondo[1]

Abstract

Virtual exchanges (VEs) based on synchronous video communication allow learners to benefit from online intercultural experiences with a high degree of interactivity (Wang, 2004). Video conferencing tools allow synchronous audio-visual and non-verbal communication as in Face-To-Face (FTF) situations (Kock, 2005), although synchronous video communication differs from FTF communication because participants are not in the same physical space during interactions. However, technological restrictions during interaction can be compensated by media users as they adapt their communication behaviour (Walsh, 2018). This is the case of the present study which analyses the use of the video camera by learners to support oral communication with the visual information present in their physical spaces. For this purpose, 50 video-recorded intercultural activities carried out by 30 pairs of undergraduate students in Spain, Ireland, Mexico, and the United States were analysed through observation techniques. Results show how Visual Supported Actions (VSAs) are a new digital non-verbal communication which supports intercultural communication in the Foreign Language (FL), blurring the contextual physical restrictions of video conferences. Moreover, the study shows that VSAs are a new way of online Self-Disclosure (SD), a process of communication through which one person reveals information about themselves to another (Sprecher et al., 2013).

---

1. Universitat Oberta de Catalunya, Barcelona, Spain; mfondo@uoc.edu; https://orcid.org/0000-0003-1181-2322

How to cite: Fondo, M. (2021). Supporting intercultural communication with visual information in virtual exchanges: when a picture paints a thousand words. In M. Satar (Ed.), *Virtual exchange: towards digital equity in internationalisation* (pp. 73-81). Research-publishing.net. https://doi.org/10.14705/rpnet.2021.53.1291

© 2021 Marta Fondo (CC BY-NC-ND)

Keywords: virtual exchange, SCMC affordances, self-disclosure, multimodal communication.

1. Introduction

Audio and videoconferencing tools have rapidly evolved from expensive equipment to computer and mobile applications (Helm, 2015). Hence, online communication tools and applications are becoming increasingly available and varied (O'Dowd, Sauro, & Spector-Cohen, 2020). This has allowed the spread of synchronous video communication in VE projects offering a closer *real-world communicative experience* to learners. Among their positive contributions, VEs support internationalisation, the development of workplace skills, and provide student-centred instruction (Nafsa, 2020). VEs also benefit oral proficiency as they boost learners' speaking skills and add a sense of purpose to collaborate with other learners (Canals, 2020). Furthermore, VEs increase the willingness to interact (Jauregi, De Graaff, van den Bergh, & Kriz, 2012), fostering intercultural communicative competence development (Jung et al., 2019). However, the effects of using videoconferencing systems to communicate in intercultural and multilingual settings remain mainly unexplored. As O'Dowd et al. (2020) state, "researchers should continue to examine the affordances and constraints of online tools" (p. 169). Hence, this study aims at exploring factors involved in the use of VSAs in VE settings and the power of image for intercultural communication.

2. Background

2.1. Videoconferencing and VEs: the effect of visual information in Synchronous Computer-mediated Communication (SCMC)

Video communication is perceived as more interactive and closer to in-person communication than other text-based or audio CMC (Liaw & Ware, 2018). As an example of affordances of the media, undergraduate students at Kern and

Develotte's (2018) exchange between Berkeley and Lyon reported having felt online videoconferencing encounters as more real than FTF because the video interlocutor was really in France and the US.

Despite all the benefits of SCMC in VE, researchers have found that multimodal communication through videoconferencing tools implies higher cognitive efforts (Kock, 2005). In the case of learners communicating in the FL, SCMC is more demanding as they need to be competent in the FL as well as "become fluent in new codes such as online speech and writing and image" (Hampel & Hauck, 2006, p. 12). Yet in 2006, O'Dowd and Ritter pointed at the challenges VE can provoke if practitioners focus on students' access to technology and not on their technological skills. In addition, problems in VEs can also arise due to language, cultural differences (Helm, 2015), and emotional factors (Fondo & Jacobetty, 2020) among students, as we will see in the following subsections.

2.2. Technological affordances and culture

Sauro and Chapelle (2017) pointed at the intersection between linguistic and cultural competences mediated by technology and used in the digital spaces and platforms where interaction between learners occurs, coining the term langua-technocultural competence. Taking into account that "affordances neither belong to the environment nor the individual, but rather to the relationship between individuals and their perceptions of environments" (Parchoma, 2014, p. 361), participants from different cultural groups could perceive the social interactive affordances provided by Information And Communication Technology (ICT) tools differently, affecting the way they use technology (Tu, 2000).

2.3. Technology and SD

Apparently, communication that has visual information (personal picture or video) in online chatting prevents the sense of anonymity so may increase inhibitions (see Nguyen, Bin, & Campbell, 2012 for a review). For instance, Brunet and Schmidt (2007) analysed conversations between unacquainted strangers. They reported that shyness was associated with the presence of webcams during online interaction, resulting in lower levels of SD. Some students may feel challenged or uncomfortable when using video in SCMC. Thus, it is not the preferred means for initial contact in VEs (Liaw & Ware, 2018).

Nevertheless, there is evidence supporting the benefits of synchronous video communication. For instance, Palloff and Pratt (2007) discovered that although written communication fostered more elaborated messages, students were more likely to feel isolated. In addition, videoconferencing tools can support interaction if learners use the affordances provided by technology for meaning-making (Satar, 2016). Then technology will help to overcome the limitations resulting from the communication in an FL with distant peers (Thorne, Cornillie, & Piet, 2012).

3. Methodology

The sample of this study is composed of 30 pairs – 60 undergraduate students – from Spain, Ireland, Mexico, and the United States. Students were involved in an online intercultural project designed and implemented in the degree of business administration in 2018 at the Universitat Oberta de Catalunya (UOC) in Spain. Spanish speakers – students at UOC and the Benemérita Universidad Autónoma de Puebla – were paired with English speakers, students at University of Limerick (Ireland), and University of Minnesota (United States). During the project, participants had five video conferences in which they carried out five different task types (ice-breaking, spot the difference, decision-making, role-play, and opinion exchange). The videoconferencing sessions were bilingual (English and Spanish).

The project from which this study stems focused on the exploration of the emotional and intercultural dimensions in VEs (see Fondo & Jacobetty, 2020). During the analysis of the qualitative data of the project (observation, transcription, and codification of students' video-recorded online sessions), a new way of communication between participants was identified. They were sharing personal information and self-disclosing through images using their portable device (laptops, tablets, and phones) or webcams, what was coined as VSAs.

For this study, a total of 50 video-recorded interactions were analysed. Thirty of them correspond to 30 pairs carrying out the first task (ice-breaking) and 20 recordings correspond to five pairs (with different personality traits) performing the subsequent four task types explained above. The analysis was based on observation and transcription of the recordings following a content analysis procedure. The transcriptions captured actions and speech and were coded using Atlas.ti with an inductive approach in an iterative process. The main categories, subcategories, and codes were reviewed by the project's expert in artificial intelligence (image and text labelling), Dr Mohammad Mahdi Dehshibi. The VSAs were finally coded under three main categories: type, mode, and subject, as explained in the following section.

To explore if the use of VSAs was related to students' profiles or only to students' use of devices, quantitative data gathered in the pre-project questionnaire (Fondo, Jacobetty, & Erdocia, 2018) was used to measure students' levels of proficiency in the FL, SD, and FL anxiety although no connections between them were found.

4. Results and discussion

VSAs were found in 12 pairs out of 30, in which 14 students out of 60 used VSA to communicate with their partners. Among the 50 interactions analysed, 13 recordings had VSAs, 12 of them occurred during the first task (ice-breaking), and only one was found in subsequent tasks.

The first category, *Type* of VSA resulted in two subcategories: *voluntary*, the speaker shows on-screen or uses something already visible to support the conversation; and *non-voluntary* provoked by (1) a Question Trigger (QT) whereby the interlocutor uses their partner's on-screen environment to ask for information or as a topic for conversation, or (2) an interruption when a person/

animal/object suddenly appears on the screen. The second category, *Mode*, differentiates between *fixed camera*, visible in the background, brought to or appearing at the camera's framework, and *dynamic camera*, when the camera or device is moved to show a person/animal/object. Finally, the category S*ubject* gathered the content of the VSAs and was divided into the subcategories *personal* and *other* (see Table 1).

Table 1. Main categories of VSA and recurrence of codes under each category

VSA main categories		
Type	**Voluntary N = 25**	
	Non-voluntary N = 8	
	Interruption	6
	QT	2
Mode	**Fix N = 20**	
	Background	6
	Brought	9
	Appears	5
	Dynamic N = 13	
Subject	Personal	29
	Other	4

Regarding VSAs' content, the most recurrent topics were family (n=11) and pets (n=7), followed by location (n=5), spare time (n=4), studies (n=3), and weather (n=3). The information shared through VSAs is more personal than expected for a first videoconference supporting the findings regarding the importance of SD to create bonds and liking (Sprecher et al., 2013). In this regard, Helm (2015) states that in VE "perhaps the greatest challenge on an interactional level though is getting students to engage in deeper levels of interaction" (p. 201). Hence, if VSAs contribute to help students feel more connected between them and confident in their communication, it could positively affect their motivation and minimise some of the common VE's setbacks explained in the introduction and background sections.

At the same time, results in this study contradict the idea of visual information as an inhibitor of SD seen in Brunet and Schmidt (2007) and Nguyen et al. (2012). On the contrary, VSAs seem to support intercultural communication in VEs, helping to share personal information and lessening communication barriers in the FL.

5. Conclusions

This study has highlighted the important role that ICT tools have in intercultural communication as a means to support conversation, as well as to share information in VEs. The affordances provided by videoconferencing tools have allowed a different way of non-verbal communication through moving images. Participants' use of videoconferencing tools trespasses spatial limitations of framed video communication, allowing VSAs to support SD by solving communication breakdowns and language limitations during intercultural communication.

In this study, it was not possible to link students' VSAs with their personality traits, culture, gender, or proficiency level obtained from the quantitative data gathered in the main project. Results, so far, seem to point at differences in students' agency of tools for communication regardless of their profile. Thus, pedagogical mentoring – providing students with the necessary support and information to succeed in VEs – will be of help (O'Dowd et al., 2020) to assure that students can benefit from the use of VSAs for intercultural communication with people from different linguistic and cultural backgrounds. If students understand the benefits of using the video camera on their devices, it could encourage them to overcome shyness and other emotional barriers related to exposure in videoconferences. Moreover, sharing examples of other VE experiences can help to raise awareness among students to understand how culture, technology, and language can interact to shape meanings in online communicative contexts (Ware, 2013).

References

Brunet P. M., & Schmidt, L. A. (2007). Is shyness context specific? Relation between shyness and online self-disclosure with and without a live webcam in young adults. *Journal of Research in Personality, 41*(4), 938-945. https://doi.org/10.1016/j.jrp.2006.09.001

Canals, L. (2020). The effects of virtual exchanges on oral skills and motivation. *Language Learning & Technology, 24*(3), 103-119. http://hdl.handle.net/10125/44742

Fondo, M., & Jacobetty, P. (2020). Exploring affective barriers in virtual exchange: the telecollaborative foreign language anxiety scale. *Journal of Virtual Exchange, 3*(SI), 37-61. https://doi.org/10.21827/jve.3.36083

Fondo, M., Jacobetty, P., & Erdocia, I. (2018). Foreign language anxiety and self-disclosure analysis as personality traits for online synchronous intercultural exchange practice. In P. Taalas, J. Jalkanen, L. Bradley & S. Thouësny (Eds), *Future-proof CALL: language learning as exploration and encounters – short papers from EUROCALL 2018* (pp. 59-63). Research-publishing.net. https://doi.org/10.14705/rpnet.2018.26.813

Hampel, R., & Hauck, M. (2006). Computer-mediated language learning: making meaning in multimodal virtual learning spaces. *The JALT CALL Journal, 2*(2), 3-18. https://doi.org/10.29140/jaltcall.v2n2.23

Helm, F. (2015). The practices and challenges of telecollaboration in higher education in Europe. *Language, Learning and Technology, 19*, 197-217.

Jauregi, K., De Graaff, R., van den Bergh, H., & Kriz, M. (2012). Native/non-native speaker interactions through video-web communication: a clue for enhancing motivation? *Computer Assisted Language Learning, 25*(1), 1-19. https://doi.org/10.1080/09588221.2011.582587

Jung, Y., Kim, Y., Lee, H., Cathey, R., Carver, J., & Skalicky, S. (2019). Learner perception of multimodal synchronous computer-mediated communication in foreign language classrooms. *Language Teaching Research, 23*(3), 287-309. https://doi.org/10.1177/1362168817731910

Kern, R., & Develotte, C. (2018). (Eds). *Screens and scenes: multimodal communication in online intercultural encounters*. Routledge. https://doi.org/10.4324/9781315447124

Kock, N. (2005). Media richness or media naturalness? The evolution of our biological communication apparatus and its influence on our behavior toward e-communication tools. *IEEE transactions on professional communication, 48*(2), 117-130.

Liaw, M.-L., & Ware, P. (2018). Multimodality and social presence in an intercultural exchange setting. In R. Kern & C. Develotte (Eds), *Screens and scenes: multimodal communication in online intercultural encounters* (pp. 256-276). Routledge. https://doi.org/10.4324/9781315447124-12

Nafsa. (2020, June 4). Virtual exchange 101. https://www.nafsa.org/ie-magazine/2020/6/4/virtual-exchange-101#:~:text=Focus%20on%20Outcomes,%2C%20and%20student%2Dcentered%20instruction

Nguyen, M., Bin, Y. S., & Campbell, A. (2012). Comparing online and offline self-disclosure: a systematic review. *Cyberpsychology, Behavior, and Social Networking, 15*(2), 103-111. https://doi.org/10.1089/cyber.2011.0277

O'Dowd, R., & Ritter, M. (2006). Understanding and working with 'failed communication' in telecollaborative exchanges. *CALICO Journal, 23*(3), 623-642. https://doi.org/10.1558/cj.v23i3.623-642

O'Dowd, R., Sauro, S., & Spector-Cohen, E. (2020). The role of pedagogical mentoring in virtual exchange. *TESOL Quaterly, 54*(1), 146-172. https://doi.org/10.1002/tesq.543

Palloff, R. M., & Pratt, K. (2007). *Building online learning communities: effective strategies for the virtual classroom*. John Wiley & Sons.

Parchoma, G. (2014). The contested ontology of affordances: implications for researching technological affordances for collaborative knowledge production. *Computers in Human Behavior, 37*, 360-368. https://doi.org/10.1016/j.chb.2012.05.028

Satar, H. M. (2016). Meaning-making in online language learner interactions via desktop videoconferencing. *ReCALL, 28*(3), 305-325. https://doi.org/10.1017/s0958344016000100

Sauro, S., & Chapelle, C. A. (2017). Toward langua-technocultural competences. In C. A. Chapelle & S. Sauro (Eds), *The handbook of technology and second language teaching and learning* (pp. 459-472). Wiley-Blackwell.

Sprecher, S., Treger, S., Wondra, J. D., Hilaire, N., & Wallpe, K. (2013). Taking turns: reciprocal self-disclosure promotes liking in initial interactions. *Journal of Experimental Social Psychology, 49*(5), 860-866. https://doi.org/10.1016/j.jesp.2013.03.017

Thorne, S. L., Cornillie, F., & Piet, D. (2012). ReCALL special issue: digital games for language learning: challenges and opportunities. *ReCALL, 24*(3), 243-256. https://doi.org/10.1017/s0958344012000134

Tu, C.-H. (2000). Critical examination of factors affecting interaction on CMC. *Journal of Network and Computer Applications, 23*(1), 39-58. https://doi.org/10.1006/jnca.1999.0100

Walsh, A. C. (2018). *"I see what you're saying": examining self-disclosure and nonverbal communication in digital environments*. 2000-2019-CSU Theses and Dissertations.

Wang, Y. (2004). Supporting synchronous distance language learning with desktop videoconferencing. *Language Learning & Technology, 8*(3), 90-121. http://www.lltjournal.org/item/2474

Ware, P. (2013). Teaching comments: intercultural communication skills in the digital age. *Intercultural Education, 24*(4), 315-326. https://doi.org/10.1080/14675986.2013.809249

Section 3.
Multisensory VE projects

7. Making the virtual tangible: using visual thinking to enhance online transnational learning

Kelly M. Murdoch-Kitt[1] and Denielle J. Emans[2]

Abstract

Tangible visual thinking activities can enrich long-distance intercultural learning experiences by improving realism, respect, and equity. This occurs through the creation of boundary objects, which can be physical objects that generate shared understanding across diverse teams and disciplinary boundaries. In the case of this study, visual thinking activities produce boundary objects in the form of visual creations – such as sketches, photographs, collages, and data visualizations. Used strategically in conjunction with Collaborative Online International Learning (COIL) curricula in any academic discipline, these activities cultivate self-reflection, communication, mutual understanding, cultural learning, and cooperative work. The benefits of visual thinking enrich and enhance transnational learning, as illustrated and observed in the course of the authors' ongoing nine-year study of Virtual Exchanges (VEs) between learners situated in the Middle East and North America. The visual thinking activities in this study complement and work in parallel with COIL curricula or existing courses that instructors have already planned. They can also occur in conjunction with regular course activities leading up to and throughout a collaboration to enhance relationship-building and trust. Visual thinking activities offer ways for learners to understand and appreciate their collaborative partnerships beyond the screen. In the

---

1. University of Michigan, Ann Arbor, United States; kmmk@umich.edu; https://orcid.org/0000-0003-3410-6017

2. Roger Williams University, Bristol, Rhode Island, United States; demans@rwu.edu; https://orcid.org/0000-0003-3185-2997

How to cite: Murdoch-Kitt, K. M., & Emans, D. J. (2021). Making the virtual tangible: using visual thinking to enhance online transnational learning. In M. Satar (Ed.), *Virtual exchange: towards digital equity in internationalisation* (pp. 85-100). Research-publishing.net. https://doi.org/10.14705/rpnet.2021.53.1292

context of long-distance intercultural experiences, the tangible and tactile nature of these activities reinforces the verisimilitude of the collaboration and its participants. After completing these preliminary activities, the study findings indicate an increase in the quality of projects that students produce together.

Keywords: visual thinking, digital equity, self-awareness, collaboration, tangible, meaningful relationships.

1. Introduction and literature review

Visual thinking is the act of making one's thoughts or ideas visible. This study examines how participants use visual thinking to formulate a deeper understanding and appreciation of self and respective intercultural partners within COIL exchanges. Activities that support visual thinking can range from sketches and prototypes, to writings and models. As tangible manifestations of visual thinking, these basic categories include thought objects, progress objects, and dialogue objects that center on the kind of communication they each support (Murdoch-Kitt & Emans, 2020). These three object categories come from the sociological construct of boundary objects, which, according to Star and Griesemer, are created objects, images, or communications that serve to facilitate understanding of communication, identity, and self-reflection (Star & Griesemer, 1989). While these visual thinking objects can be seen as a form of visual communication, in this study they are less formal and personalized to team communications, whereas the field of visual communication is generally more concerned with communicating to wider audiences.

While VE prioritizes cultural learning and sharing, COIL prioritizes collaboration on project-based learning outcomes between participants from different cultural backgrounds and geographic locations. Long-distance intercultural learning has long been a topic of interest within various academic disciplines. While

Rubin and his team coined the term COIL in 2004 (Rubin, 2018), providing a shared lexicon to describe VE, there remains a need to embed visual thinking in international co-teaching and co-learning strategies. As evidenced by the focus on technological translation tools and logistics in the current VE literature, visual thinking as a pedagogical VE methodology remains an underutilized means of creating and exchanging information, and of relationship-building among COIL participants.

The literature discusses some projects that utilize an emic approach, which helps students gain an insider's perspective into a partner culture. Yet, literature overwhelmingly focuses on logistics (Pearl & Verruck, 2019) and the use of tools (Simon, 2019). With few exceptions (e.g. Schadewitz, 2009, which delves into some design 'patterns'), discussions around communication often emphasize technology use as paramount to establishing connections between participants (as in Wilmot, Rushton, & Hofmann, 2016). In order to fully support intercultural learning and collaboration beyond tools, logistics, and technology, instructors have a responsibility to introduce communication strategies and interpersonal competencies into their pedagogies. Though widely overlooked in the COIL literature, visual communication is an effective strategy for engaging participants in understanding each other's lived experiences.

Visual communication can serve as a rather universal language to deepen dialogues and connections beyond the tip of Hall's (1976) theoretical cultural iceberg. As evidenced in prior academic research, the need to develop effective communication competencies is heightened when teammates work together globally *and* remotely (Bennett, Eglash, & Krishnamoorthy, 2011). Evolving technology offers potential for richer exchanges, but brings its own barriers and is not necessarily ubiquitous. In pursuit of critical telecollaboration, VE classrooms also need to go beyond typical icebreaker activities or superficial connections, which sometimes fail to develop a critical understanding of the self or others (O'Dowd, 2016). These surface-level interactions, such as discussions of cuisines, can unwittingly reinforce cultural stereotypes by offering a shortsighted view of a particular country, culture, or people.

Chapter 7

Because creating and sharing ideas through images can encourage comprehension of complex ideas (Nelson & Stolterman, 2014), promote negotiation (Singh, 2011), and enable dialogue (Tharp & Tharp, 2018), visual thinking has many positive effects on VE. *Boundary objects* support this process, enabling learners to exchange knowledge and co-create by navigating compromises and encouraging dialogue, trust-building, and understanding (Leonard-Barton, 1995; Star & Griesemer, 1989; Takeuchi & Nonaka, 1995). Boundary objects can be physical objects that generate shared understanding across diverse teams and disciplinary boundaries. Visual, product, and interactive design, as well as other creative disciplines, commonly use boundary objects as forms of visual thinking – to explain or express thoughts, elicit feedback, build upon ideas, and reach consensus (Marheineke, 2016).

Together, these positive attributes of visual thinking and communication help promote equity among intercultural collaborators as a result of individuals' in-depth perspective-taking by making, exchanging, and interpreting each other's visual thinking objects. According to the US-based National Digital Inclusion Alliance[3], while digital inclusion entails providing access to hardware, software, internet access, and other technical resources, one of its key aims is "to enable and encourage self-sufficiency, participation and collaboration". To that end, visual objects help individuals understand themselves and their partners more deeply by inviting more sophisticated and critical conversations. This involves creating space for each other, more attentive listening, and the ability to embrace differences as opposed to seeking commonalities. Over the course of this ten-year study, this has been evidenced in the complexity and perspectives present in teams' project outcomes and is overwhelmingly noted in students' individual written reflections of their experience.

This ongoing study builds on previous work in multisensory and tangible approaches to international education and co-learning. Creating and engaging with visual and physical objects has proven effective in a range of areas, such as language learning; for example, where beginner English learners utilize

---

3. https://www.digitalinclusion.org/definitions

'tactile, visual, and kinetic' means to thoughtfully connect images and image-making with language (Gorjian, Hayati, & Barazandeh, 2012). Meanwhile, a study that used drawing to engage and connect medical and fine art students in 'critical looking' shows how visual communication promotes interdisciplinary communication and learning (Lyon, Letschka, Ainsworth, & Haq, 2013). These examples show the efficacy of visual thinking in diverse contexts. Its tactile and physical components help students feel more connected to their work and teammates. However, these examples rely on in-person interactions. The authors extend the findings from these studies into the virtual learning realm and, specifically, the practice of COIL. An overview of positive outcomes discussed in this paper encourages educators to incorporate visual thinking strategies within COIL curricula.

2. Methodology

2.1. Constructive-developmental paradigm

This research utilized constructive-developmental theory (Baxter Magolda, 2001; Kegan, 1994) and grounded theory (Charmaz, 2014; Glaser, 1978) to analyze and compare the qualitative data collected over the course of the study. This form of data collection involved classroom observations, student questionnaires, student written reflections, and project outcomes. As part of this process, the constructive-developmental theory promotes the cultivation of students' self-understanding as a precursor to understanding others. This theory is critical to COIL, with boundary objects assisting in this developmental progression.

Applying these theories to an ongoing series of VE, the authors developed more than 30 visual thinking activities to support COIL. These activities were developed from 2011 to present between different cohorts of students based in North America and the Middle East. Using observations and qualitative online questionnaires to obtain feedback and to continually improve upon the activities, the authors have so far prototyped, tested, and refined these activities with over 300 students hailing from 23 different countries.

Chapter 7

Findings indicate the visual thinking activities are effective in both COIL curricula and classrooms that are not part of VE. Some of the authors' tactile visual thinking activities include the Teamthink Constellation; Picture Story Shuffle; Cultural Icebergs; Comparative Impression Maps; Belief Brainstorm; Datastorming; and value collage (Murdoch-Kitt & Emans, 2020). This paper focuses specifically on the value collage activity (see Figure 1), which demonstrates the theories of the constructive-developmental paradigm and boundary objects.

2.2. Value collage

The value collage activity asks participants to consider where their own values come from and then write lists of their personal and cultural values. Next, they explore how to represent these values visually using various materials or media to make a *collage*, a tactile visual composition created from selecting, combining, and arranging cut-out images, colors, textures, and text. Because of the open-ended nature of the prompt and because it is informed by each individual's values, each completed value collage is unique. Instructors encourage students to create their collages by hand, however, some end up creating digital compositions, or combining physical materials into a digital composition.

In creating, sharing, and discussing collages – first with collocated classmates, then with international partners – through synchronous and asynchronous means, the activity enables individuals to better understand themselves and prepare for thoughtful conversations with COIL partners. For example, in response to the value collage activity, one US-based participant wrote,

> "I hadn't thought about how culture could influence your values and it really forced me to dig deeper into how my identity and culture correlates with these values I hold most important".

This self-reflective aspect of learning is critical to building trust and long-term relationships between participants, and visual thinking enhances self-reflection.

Kelly M. Murdoch-Kitt and Denielle J. Emans

Figure 1. Example value collages[4]; this activity is effective in both COIL and non-exchange courses alike. As with these examples, the activity can be conducted using physical materials (e.g. magazine cut-outs), digital images, or a combination of both

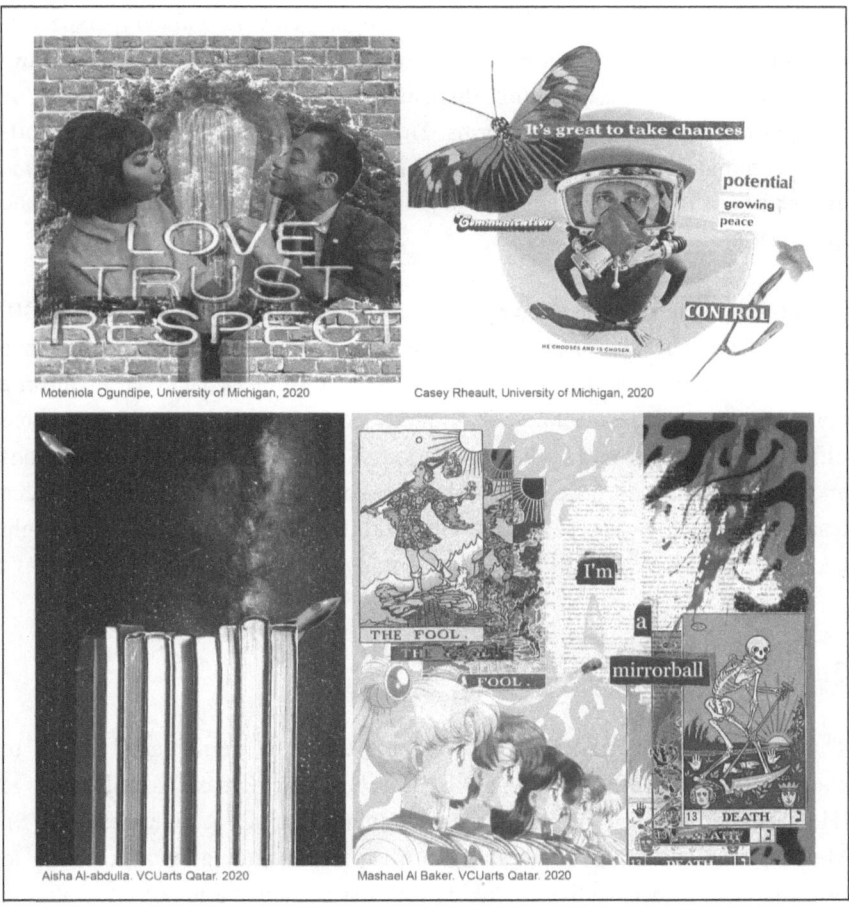

4. We have not been able to follow up with the participating students to ensure all the images used in their collages are copyright-free. We nevertheless believe all of the work – as is typical with collage – falls within the fair use doctrine as 'transformative' work, which states: "transformative uses take the original copyrighted work and transform its appearance or nature to such a high degree that the use no longer qualifies as infringing". In this way, the collages bring together various images to speak about each person's personal value systems.

Chapter 7

2.3. Communication methods

Throughout the process, instructors guide students in discussions between collocated classmates as a precursor to sharing with long-distance intercultural partners. This internal discussion boosts confidence, promotes individual self-reflection, and provides practice dialogue. Having gained perspective on their own values, they are then better able to appreciate their classmates' and collaborators' values. Within this study, discussions of participants' value collages have taken a variety of forms. This is because each of the COIL cohorts have communicated with each other through a variety of synchronous and asynchronous methods, depending on the nature of particular collaboration and the constraints of the semester.

Sometimes, when courses have been scheduled at compatible times, COIL partners have a great deal of synchronous discussion (e.g. live videoconference meetings) and are able to share and discuss their value collages in a real-time conversation. In other cases, such as study cohorts with 11- to 12-hour time differences, asynchronous communications such as messaging applications and email exchanges have been the dominant mode of conversing between teammates. In this case, a discussion about individuals' value collages might take place over several days' time.

3. Discussion

The authors characterize *meaningful relationships* by participants' ability to cooperate and work efficiently with each other based on increased social exchange (Homans, 1958) and reduced social uncertainty (Berger & Calabrese, 1975). Meaningful relationships are built upon trust, understanding, and the ability to listen to others' perspectives. Making and exchanging various visual objects – such as sketches, photographs, collages, drawings, and data visualizations – helps VE participants open up to new perspectives and take them into account (Murdoch-Kitt & Emans, 2020). When these activities are integrated into COIL projects, participants become equipped to foster and sustain meaningful relationships. For example, survey data revealed that 60% of the authors' most recent COIL cohort would stay in touch with their global collaborators following the project completion. Additionally, 72% stated an increased interest in future intercultural opportunities.

When asked to respond in writing to this question, *What would you tell another student who is thinking about enrolling in this course?*, one participant noted:

> "If they are looking for an experience where they'll understand themselves and others better by the end of it then this is for them. If they want experience in collaboration or with meeting new people from different places and of different backgrounds then this course is definitely right up their alley".

Another participant stated:

> "This is a great opportunity to build collaboration, communication, research, and critical thinking skills".

Going beyond initial ice-breakers and surface-level communications, visual thinking activities and resulting boundary objects can support collaborators in project-based learning. During tactile visual activities like the value collage, the physical aspects of combining various elements together into a single image become visual signifiers of the various students participating in VE. Students reflect openly on values depicted in their own and their partners' collages, revisiting these throughout their collaboration. This shared experience is a worthwhile and engaging way to understand people, beyond simply connecting via social media or asynchronous small talk (Murdoch-Kitt & Emans, 2020).

As one COIL participant in the study wrote in a freewriting response following the value collage activity:

> "I don't think I've really ever considered where these values came from and how they are influenced by the context/culture in which I live.

> As humans, we have a tendency to find comfort in familiarity, and discourse on the value discrepancies between people and cultures can be even more uncomfortable in many respects because our values dictate so much of who we are. The idea of channeling these conversations through a different medium to help lessen the personal baggage and invite inquiry is a really cool idea and makes me wonder how we could reframe other potentially difficult/uncomfortable topics to facilitate these important conversations".

Qualitative data collected from the authors' study reveal that visual thinking activities positively affect the majority of students' participation and engagement in COIL. The activities captivate the senses and push students to think creatively and critically about who they are as individuals, enhancing their experience with project-based learning. For instance, one participant noted in their weekly reflection, in response to the question 'who are we':

> "I think the value collage made me think a lot about what values I hold in general and what things I actually uphold in my own life. I think there is a little bit of a disconnect there and it's important to acknowledge that and again take a closer analysis of what is most important to who I am individually. I think who 'we' are as a whole is hard to define and that makes me happy! Even looking at our beliefs activity from class today it was very interesting to see the wide range of thought processes and ideas that I hadn't even thought of".

When these activities are done by hand – using physical materials including paper, markers, string, or glue – they stimulate multiple senses and help learners appreciate the tangible reality of otherwise virtual collaborations. These findings are consistent with theories of multisensory and multichannel learning, which emphasize that utilizing different senses stimulates brain activity (Mayer, 2002; Willis, 2006). With this in mind, the ability to work with tangible materials in one's physical environment helps otherwise virtual relationships to feel less abstract to participants.

4. Benefits and challenges

A persistent challenge within COIL exchanges is the need to move beyond simply 'connecting' with others, and instead, conceive of communicative, coordinated, and cooperative partnerships. True collaborations are built on trust and openness. Thus, students must learn and employ interpersonal skills like active listening, negotiation, and patience. Systematically initiating and taking responsibility for their individual and collective roles also builds harmonious and efficient relationships.

Because the visual activities in this study are based on constructive-developmental theory, they help participants overcome surface-level assumptions and interactions. Initial introspection provides a basis for sensitive inquiry and communication with VE partners. While earnest collaboration is challenging to accomplish during VE, relationships become stronger through the shared development of a project, which relies upon and simultaneously builds interpersonal communication skills and teammates' sense of empowerment (Hill, Brandeau, Truelove, & Lineback, 2014). Beyond communication alone, visual thinking activities can support students in developing relationships around topics related to global challenges, such as defending human rights or preserving natural resources. This approach must be deliberately introduced and nourished.

Visual thinking activities like the value collage are not confined to the creative disciplines. These activities can also complement and work in parallel with existing courses or COIL curricula. These points are reinforced by Vazquez (1981), who explains that "to use art in the language classroom does not mean to teach art, but to teach language through art" (p. 1).

Finally, based on the authors' analysis of their overall observation and interpretation of this ten-year COIL study, when compared to COIL, activities improve the quality of projects that the students create together (Murdoch-Kitt & Emans, 2020). Analyzing the qualitative data about participant experience over time has enabled the study to improve upon and refine the activities as an

Chapter 7

outcome of this research. In this study, the authors observed stark differences in the working processes and outcomes of teams who employ these methods compared to those who do not use them (for example, as shown in Figure 2).

Figure 2. This representative set of participant responses about superficial similarities and differences between a team's two cities came from a cohort that did not employ any of the preliminary visual thinking activities. Below: as a result of using visual thinking early in their team-building process, two participant responses from a later cohort illustrate the heightened understanding of cultural complexity within team discussions and project topics

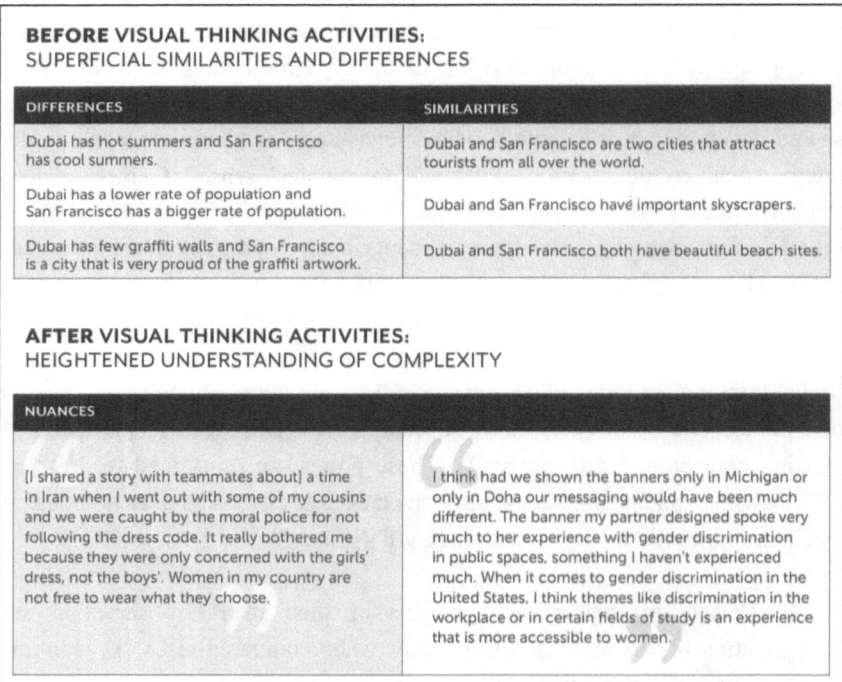

The tangible and tactile nature of visual thinking activities strengthens the verisimilitude of virtual relationships and collaborations. In other words, "tangible objects help teams build relationships, trust, and ideas" (Murdoch-Kitt & Emans, 2020, p. 225). The tangible aspects of creating boundary objects can enrich a COIL exchange by improving realism, which, in turn, improves respect and equity among participants. Research shows that equitable teams, in which members feel comfortable exchanging ideas, do better work (Leonard-Barton, 1995).

5. Conclusion

VE instructors must take responsibility to craft a plan that continually nurtures relationship-building throughout a COIL exchange. Integrating multiple strategies – including visual thinking – is key to building and maintaining important relationships that develop during this expansive process. Although VE instructors may initially perceive these activities as outside the scope of their course, visual thinking activities can enhance existing pedagogical structures, strengthening their original intent. When incorporated strategically, their ability to enhance comprehension and engagement can further reduce stresses and extra work for instructors. This is because boundary objects generate conversation around and about the artifact, rather than directly asking participants to share their beliefs, thoughts, or ideas through written or oral means alone.

The object, therefore, serves as a facilitation tool to initiate conversation among teammates and eases pressure on the students to always think on their feet or feel scrutinized by their partners as a representative of their country or culture. Deep discussions evolve around the visual objects that effectively draw out stories, perspectives and experiences which would not otherwise emerge, perhaps particularly in the presence of a lingering instructor. Instead, the VE instructor's energy can shift to supporting the cohort as a whole by introducing visual thinking activities that guide the overall COIL journey, and shift the onus of critical conversations to the students, mediated by their visual objects. As an adaptable approach, creating and working with boundary objects also levels playing fields for participants who speak different languages or feel less confident in a common instructional language. With these benefits in mind, the authors invite the IVEC community to integrate visual thinking activities to create more equitable, inclusive, and meaningful relationships among their VE cohorts.

References

Baxter Magolda, M. B. (2001). *Making their own way: narratives for transforming higher education to promote self-development.* Stylus.

Bennett, A., Eglash, R., & Krishnamoorthy, M. (2011). Virtual design studio: facilitating online learning and communication between U.S. and Kenyan participants. In K. St. Amant & F. Sapienza (Eds), *Culture, communication, and cyberspace: rethinking technical communication for international online environments* (pp. 183-206). Routledge.

Berger, C. R., & Calabrese, R. J. (1975). Some explorations in initial interaction and beyond: toward a developmental theory of interpersonal communication. *Human Communication Research, 1*(2), 99-112. https://doi.org/10.1111/j.1468-2958.1975.tb00258.x

Charmaz, K. (2014). *Constructing grounded theory.* Sage Publications.

Glaser, B. (1978). *Theoretical sensitivity: advances in the methodology of grounded theory.* The Sociology Press.

Gorjian, B., Hayati, A., & Barazandeh, E. (2012). An evaluation of the effects of art on vocabulary learning through multi-sensory modalities. *Procedia Technology, 1,* 345-350. https://doi.org/10.1016/j.protcy.2012.02.072

Hall, E. T. (1976). *Beyond culture.* Anchor Books.

Hill, L. A., Brandeau, G., Truelove, E., & Lineback, K. (2014). *Collective genius: the art and practice of leading innovation.* Harvard Business Review Press.

Homans, G. C. (1958). Social behavior as exchange. *American Journal of Sociology, 63*(6), 597-606. https://doi.org/10.1086/222355

Kegan, R. (1994). *In over our heads: the mental demands of modern life.* Harvard University Press.

Leonard-Barton, D. (1995). *Wellsprings of knowledge: building and sustaining the sources of innovation.* Harvard Business School Press.

Lyon, P., Letschka, P., Ainsworth, T., & Haq, I. (2013). An exploratory study of the potential learning benefits for medical students in collaborative drawing: creativity, reflection and 'critical looking'. *BMC Medical Education, 13*(1), 86. https://doi.org/10.1186/1472-6920-13-86

Marheineke, M. (2016). *Designing boundary objects for virtual collaboration.* Springer Fachmedien Wiesbaden. https://doi.org/10.1007/978-3-658-15386-1

Mayer, R. E. (2002). Multimedia Learning. In *Psychology of Learning and Motivation, 41,* 85-139. https://doi.org/10.1016/S0079-7421(02)80005-6

Murdoch-Kitt, K. M., & Emans, D. J. (2020). *Intercultural collaboration by design: drawing from differences, distances, and disciplines through visual thinking.* Routledge. https://doi.org/10.4324/9780429268823

Nelson, H. G., & Stolterman, E. (2014). *The design way: intentional change in an unpredictable world.* The MIT Press.

O'Dowd, R. (2016). Emerging trends and new directions in telecollaborative learning. *Calico journal, 33*(3), 291-310.

Pearl, M., & Verruck, F. (2019). Internationalization at home and virtual team collaboration meet global challenges: a practical approach to international business. *2019 International Virtual Exchange Conference (IVEC) Proceedings* (pp. 46-50). http://iveconference.org/wp-content/uploads/2019/12/IVEC-2019-Conference-Proceedings.pdf

Rubin, J. (2018). The collaborative online international learning network: online intercultural exchange in the state university of New York network of Universities. In R. O'Dowd & T. Lewis (Eds), *Online intercultural exchange: policy, pedagogy, practice* (pp. 263-272). Routledge. https://doi.org/10.4324/9781315678931

Schadewitz, N. (2009). Design patterns for cross-cultural collaboration. *International Journal of Design, 3*(3).

Simon, N. (2019). Choosing the best technology for your COIL project. *2019 International Virtual Exchange Conference (IVEC) Proceedings* (pp. 83-89). http://iveconference.org/wp-content/uploads/2019/12/IVEC-2019-Conference-Proceedings.pdf

Singh, A. (2011). Visual artefacts as boundary objects in participatory research paradigm. *Journal of Visual Art Practice, 10*(1), 35-50. https://doi.org/10.1386/jvap.10.1.35_1

Star, S. L., & Griesemer, J. R. (1989). Institutional ecology, 'translations' and boundary objects: amateurs and professionals in Berkeley's Museum of Vertebrate Zoology, 1907-39. *Social Studies of Science, 19*(3), 387-420. https://doi.org/10.1177/030631289019003001

Takeuchi, H., & Nonaka, I. (1995). *The knowledge-creating company: how Japanese companies create the dynamics of innovation.* Oxford University Press.

Tharp, B. M., & Tharp, S. M. (2018). *Discursive design: critical, speculative, and alternative things.* The MIT Press. https://doi.org/10.7551/mitpress/11192.001.0001

Vazquez, D. (1981). Teaching a second language through art. *Writing Across the Curriculum, 1*. https://teachersinstitute.yale.edu/curriculum/guides/1981/4/81.04.12.x.html

Willis, J. (2006). *Research-based strategies to ignite student learning: insights from a neurologist and classroom teacher*. Association for Supervision and Curriculum Development.

Wilmot, N. V., Rushton, D., & Hofmann, A. S. Z. (2016). Reaching across continents: engaging students through virtual collaborations. *Higher Education Pedagogies, 1*(1), 121-139. https://doi.org/10.1080/23752696.2016.1216325

8. Virtual exchange facilitated by interactive, digital, cultural artefacts: communities, languages, and activities app (ENACT)

Colin B. Dodds[1], Alison Whelan[2], Ahmed Kharrufa[3], and Müge Satar[4]

Abstract

This chapter is based on a workshop at IVEC 2020 which presented a model of Virtual Exchange (VE) facilitated by interactive, digital, and cultural artefacts created using a progressive web app developed by the EU-funded ENACT project team. The model offers an innovative approach to online intercultural exchange through the opportunity to create, share, appropriate, and re-create cultural artefacts. Drawing on Thorne's (2016) concept of cultural artefacts, the app is designed to enable artefacts as catalysts for intercultural exchange while "artifacts and humans together create particular morphologies of action" (p. 189). The ENACT project aims to develop Open Educational Resources (OER) that will foster intergenerational and intercultural understanding within and between communities; promote opportunities for intergenerational, intercultural interaction; and offer a real-world, immersive learning experience that brings culture to life. The web app is built on the well-established H5P.org interactive media engine tailored for the

---

1. Newcastle University, Newcastle upon Tyne, United Kingdom; c.dodds2@newcastle.ac.uk; https://orcid.org/0000-0001-8225-356X

2. Newcastle University, Newcastle upon Tyne, United Kingdom; alison.whelan2@newcastle.ac.uk; https://orcid.org/0000-0001-6272-6497

3. Newcastle University, Newcastle upon Tyne, United Kingdom; ahmed.kharrufa@newcastle.ac.uk; https://orcid.org/0000-0002-3461-4161

4. Newcastle University, Newcastle upon Tyne, United Kingdom; muge.satar@newcastle.ac.uk; https://orcid.org/0000-0002-2382-6740

How to cite: Dodds, C. B., Whelan, A., Kharrufa, A., & Satar, M. (2021). Virtual exchange facilitated by interactive, digital, cultural artefacts: communities, languages, and activities app (ENACT). In M. Satar (Ed.), *Virtual exchange: towards digital equity in internationalisation* (pp. 101-112). Research-publishing.net. https://doi.org/10.14705/rpnet.2021.53.1293

creation of, and engagement with interactive digital media for task-based exchange of cultural activities promoting linguistic, digital, and intercultural communication skills development. This chapter outlines how the ENACT app can be implemented in VE at higher education to facilitate deeper, immersive, virtual intercultural exchange experiences that go beyond talking about culture and that offer hands-on cultural experiences based on learning by doing to ensure equitable experiences to all students.

Keywords: open educational resources, ENACT app, cultural artefacts, immersive virtual exchange, virtual exchange for teacher education.

1. Introduction

The ENACT project[5] aims to develop OER that will foster intergenerational and intercultural understanding within and between communities; promote opportunities for intergenerational, intercultural interaction; and offer a real-world, immersive learning experience that brings culture and language to life. The web app is built on the well-established H5P.org interactive media engine tailored for the creation of and engagement with interactive digital media for task-based exchange of cultural activities promoting linguistic, digital, and intercultural communication skills development. It is freely available to anyone in the world, which is expected to support equal digital access to the exploration and creation of cultural content around the globe.

The ENACT project has three main goals. First, we aim to promote two-way knowledge exchange (language, culture, digital skills) and understanding between either host/migrant communities in local languages (intercultural exchange) or youth/senior members of migrant communities in heritage languages (intergenerational exchange). Second, we support the inclusion of

---

5. https://enacteuropa.com/

university students in the local community by allocating various roles to higher education students in the project activities. Finally, we offer an innovative task-based digital pedagogy for learning and VE between communities worldwide. Our workshop explored the final aim of the incorporation of the ENACT web app in VE projects in higher education.

This chapter introduces the ENACT project and examines how we presented it to transnational participants during the conference, and how we engaged them in interactive activities in order to experience the web app and understand its context.

2. Background and research aims

In this workshop, we proposed that the ENACT web app can act as a tool to trigger social interaction and intercultural dialogue in VE as it enables learners to create, share, appropriate, re-create, and engage with digital interactive cultural artefacts from various cultures. Such cultural digital artefacts can involve introducing others how to dance a specific dance, such as English Morris dancing, how to create certain cultural arts and crafts, such as making a Japanese origami boat, or activities for a specific festival, such as making a Chinese lantern to celebrate the Chinese New Year.

Theoretically, ENACT draws on Thorne's (2016) concept of artefacts and sees the digital artefacts created and shared on the web app as catalysts for intercultural exchange while "artifacts and humans together create particular morphologies of action" (Thorne, 2016, p. 189). On the one hand, we see the web app as a digital medium to facilitate the exchange of languages and cultures at two levels: engagement and creation. First, through engagement with the various features of the web app, people can learn about other languages and cultures presented via the content of the digital artefact. Second, the web app can mediate presentation and expression of one's own languages and cultures facilitated by the content creation steps of the app. On the other hand, we acknowledge that the web app itself has agency in creating and producing certain "culturally organized systems of activity" (Thorne, 2016, p. 189) through the various affordances it embodies. Thus, technological objects are not perceived as passive tools, but as social actors (Latour, 1996). This perspective enables us to understand the synergies between our design of the app, its affordances, the intercultural exchanges it facilitates, and various representations (artefacts) of cultural activities produced by different communities using the web app.

As Smith and González-Lloret (2020) argue, a language learning software or app "conveys or is at least consistent with, a certain teaching approach, which actively shapes what the teacher and/or user can do with it" (p. 2). The pedagogical design of the ENACT web app is based on task-based language teaching principles. In language learning and teaching, tasks aim "to create a real purpose for language use and to provide a natural context for language study" (Willis, 1996, p. 1). Following task-based language teaching criteria proposed by Ellis (2003), the ENACT web app enables learners to complete cultural activities using the target language, engage in social interaction while exploring or creating these cultural activities, and focus on linguistic form while being engaged in meaningful interaction.

3. Operationalising the theory

Based on the above discussion, we established two design principles for the ENACT web app: first, its key role in creating 'morphologies of action' in the learning process (Thorne, 2016), and second that this role should be structured within task-based language teaching pedagogy (Smith & González-Lloret, 2020). In task-based language teaching, tasks comprise three stages: pre-task, main task, and post-task (language focus) (Willis, 1996). The pre-task introduces the topic and task, and highlights useful words and phrases. This prepares the learners and helps them understand the task instructions. The main part of the task cycle, or what we refer to as 'main task', is the part where learners do the task individually or in small groups. Finally, the language focus, or 'post-task' is when learners practise the new words introduced in the activity, order the activity creation steps, answer questions on content, and reflect on task accomplishment and engage with other users through comments.

Before deciding on developing our own tool, we first explored the possibility of using existing tools that allow the creation of, and engagement with, interactive digital media. We are not aware of any tools that particularly scaffold user design of cultural activities within a simple task-based language learning framework, and especially ones that allow the creation of, in addition to engaging with, interactive content. *Linguacuisine* (Seedhouse, Heslop, & Kharrufa, 2020), while designed for task-based language learning, is dedicated to cooking, and the structure and level of interactivity provided is limited and lacks the flexibility required for this project. As such, we investigated H5P.org as it is a well-established, free, and open-source general interactive content engine. It offers a wide range of multimedia content types including games, quizzes, questionnaires, slide shows, and interactive videos among others. The downside is that H5P simply offers a way to create isolated interactive activities from a long list of interactive media types with no scaffolding for the choice of suitable media types.

We ran exploratory workshops with a total 42 participants (with home and migrant communities) in four countries (UK, Finland, Turkey, and Spain) following the same format in each (Dodds et al., 2020). The goal of these workshops was to carry out a preliminary appraisal of the support needed for the participants in terms of engaging with, structuring, and creating interactive tasks using the H5P.org platform directly. Among the key findings from these workshops were that H5P.org is not a suitable tool due to its lack of structure and scaffolding leaving participants struggling in terms of how to present their cultural activity. As such, what is needed is a system that provides a pedagogical structure to the content creation process to guide the content creators to produce more useful content for learners. The system should also only make available to content creators a subset of the large set of functionalities available in a tool such as H5P. The focus should be on what supports the creation of meaningful, learning focused task-based language learning activities.

4. Development of web app

The H5P engine can function as a plugin that integrates into content management systems including WordPress, Drupal, and Moodle. We opted to work with Drupal 7 because it is well supported by the H5P community and because it supports content authoring without having to give full administrative privileges to all potential users as is the case with some other systems. We then followed standard programming practices to turn our Drupal 7 site into a progressive web application which makes it look and feel like an app on mobile or tablet devices.

An area we were keen to improve concerned the H5P content authoring workflow. In a typical H5P use case, no overall task structure is provided and the content author needs to select a content type from the long list of all available H5P content types. Authors create their content, taking advantage of the customisation facilities to adapt the look and feel of their content. Such workflow offers great flexibility and is well suited to teachers who are prepared to invest some time and effort in acquainting themselves with the H5P system and who want to apply their own pedagogies. However, we desired a workflow that channelled users towards producing content aligned with task-based language teaching pedagogy, and removed any unnecessary complexity to support non-expert users (whether from technology or pedagogy perspectives).

Our solution was to create a new H5P content type which wrapped together selected existing content types in a three-stage structure. Within this new content type, we present text instructions to guide content authors for each stage. For example, the pre-task stage starts with the introduction instruction: *Select a media type from the menu below and use it to create an introduction giving a sense of the activity's context* and a drop-down box where the user can select one of only two relevant H5P content types (for this step): interactive video or virtual tour (360 degrees). Modifications were made to some of the H5P content types we integrated into our application to better suit our language learning aims. For example, image hotspots were deemed useful for vocabulary training at the pre-task stage as an image could have 'hotspots' placed over depicted vocabulary items, and clicking a hotspot would pop-up a box revealing the associated word in textual form.

Figure 1. Affordances of the ENACT web app to focus on form

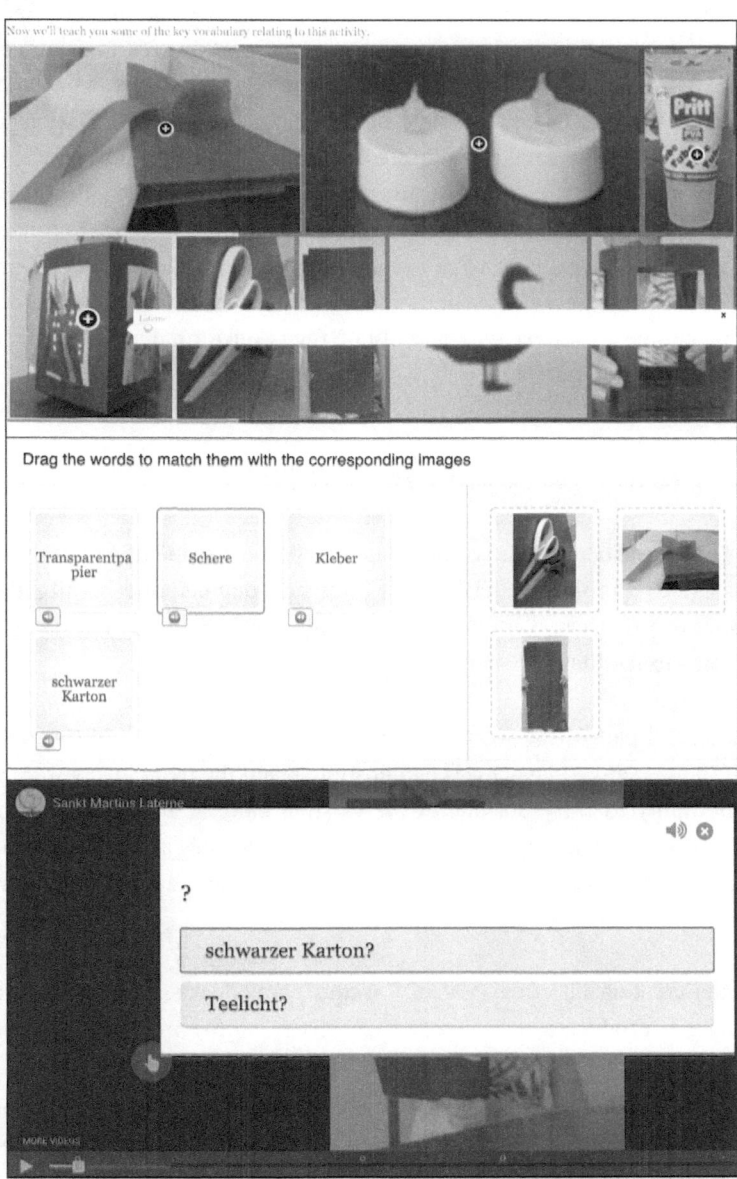

We extended this to support audio recordings for each hotspot to allow end users to hear the associated pronunciation. Similarly, an image matching content type was modified to create a game where images are paired with their textual and auditory representations to be used to practise vocabulary at the post-task stage. In addition to instructions at the content creation phase, scaffolding text was added to the presentation side of our H5P content type (i.e. the learning phase) to contextualise the wrapped content. For example, the line *Now we'll teach you some of the key vocabulary relating to this activit* is used to introduce the vocabulary training content. During the main task stage, the interactive video option enables content creators to include pop-up multiple choice questions, which facilitate focus-on-form during the meaning-focused activity (Figure 1).

5. ENACT Workshop at IVEC 2020

The IVEC workshop had three parts. The first part consisted of a brief overview of the ENACT project, describing its aims and outputs, and highlighting its relevance to VE. There was a focus on the ways in which the project outputs can be adopted to facilitate VE in higher education.

In the second part of the workshop, the engagement interface of the web app (ENACT Interactive Player) was demonstrated, and the participants were given an opportunity to carry out one of the existing cultural activities available in Turkish, Chinese, and English. The web app also includes an online community interface (ENACT Community), on which the participants can post a multimodal response to the activity they have carried out.

Next, the creation interface (ENACT Author) was discussed, and participants were able to produce a short interactive activity on the web app, and explore potentials to create immersive virtual cultural experiences by using 360 degree cameras and Google Cardboard virtual reality headsets. This part of the workshop involved a group discussion which facilitated reflection on potential applications of the ENACT web app in participants' own contexts. One of the participants later reflected how the opportunity to create an activity had made him consider how he could incorporate the app into his course in Austria. His feedback described how he envisaged using the ENACT web app to facilitate his students, based in the USA, to experience living in Vienna in a meaningful way. Other participants commented how quick and simple it was to create an activity that provided an interactive, engaging language learning experience.

By the end of the workshop, participants had learned how to use the app, and developed an understanding of how innovative technologies can facilitate deeper, immersive virtual intercultural exchange experiences that go beyond talking about culture and that offer hands-on cultural experiences based on learning by doing. There were positive comments from participants about both the enjoyment and engagement aspect of the app, such as one transnational participant who commented: "I participated in your workshop on the ENACT app. My colleague and I would like to thank you again for a great session, where we both learned a lot and enjoyed having the opportunity to use your new app!". There was also feedback on how the app could be used in an academic context to facilitate cultural immersion within an international programme: "one of our main goals for the course is to help students experience our city in a meaningful way, virtually. We think the ENACT app would be a great way to facilitate this".

Comments were added to the activities on the web app after the workshop, which demonstrated the participants' engagement, with feedback including, "it was really interesting to learn new vocabulary and sentences while engaging in a fun activity. I am sure that I will now remember the words better than if I would have only read a text or listened to an audio file". This gave us an idea of which aspects of the app were proving successful and how participants viewed their experience. However, some participants experienced challenges in the creation of the cultural activity in terms of technical development and ease of use. These are especially important aspects when implementing the web app as a tool for VE ensuring learners can support each other technically since not all learners have equal levels of digital skills, which is essential in providing equitable learning experiences for all.

6. Using the ENACT web app for VE

University instructors interested in introducing interculturality in their teaching and learning can use the ENACT web app as part of their VE to support internationalisation at higher education. For example, pilot implementations were planned for the fall semester of the 2020-2021 academic year at two project partner institutions: Newcastle University and Universitat Autònoma de Barcelona.

At Newcastle University, the ENACT web app was implemented within an existing three-week VE with pre-service language teachers in the UK and Turkey. The purpose of the exchange was to offer experiential practice in VE to teacher trainees of Teaching of English to Speaker of Other Languages (TESOL). The cultural activities on the ENACT app were used as a springboard to prompt intercultural dialogue to further participants' understanding of culture(s), cultural objects, and cultural activities. In intercultural groups, the participants then used the ENACT web app to choose and digitally co-create a cultural activity that they choose while communicating synchronously via videoconferencing. We asked teacher trainees to complete individual e-portfolio entries at the end of each task to explore deeper understandings of culture and language learning gains, but also to identify challenges in using the ENACT web app for online intercultural exchange. Some learner comments from their e-portfolios were as follows:

> "when we talked about our culture, I learned some words and activities from Saudi Arabia and Czech Republic. For example, fishing is a cultural activity in Saudi Arabia and fish means 'smak' in Arabic. Also, I learned the word 'kroj' which means 'costume' so; I learned both a word and a national costume of Czech Republic".

> "I liked when we talked about the sense of belonging and whether each one of us feels that we have it or now and to what level we can relate to other cultures or to our own".

"when uploading materials, [name of another participant] was waiting for my email while I thought she had received it and at that time we were all waiting for the materials to be upload [sic]. We had waited nearly half an hour before realising we got each other wrong. This funny misunderstanding shows that it's the same in both of our cultures not to urge others, because that might suggest you have no confidence or patience in him/her, and thus make you feel impolite".

"my Turkish partners told us that in some parts of Turkey, people used various methods to make the bride cry at the wedding, and then they danced together. I've never heard of such cultural activity before, and I thought it was very special and interesting. I am very happy to have this opportunity to learn about the cultural activities in Turkey, which is very meaningful".

7. Conclusion

In this chapter we described a workshop which provided a model of VE facilitated by interactive, digital, cultural artefacts. These artefacts were created, shared, and engaged with through the ENACT web app and will persist as OER. As the ENACT project progresses, so too will the opportunities to foster intergenerational and intercultural understanding within and between communities, to promote opportunities for intergenerational, intercultural interaction, to and offer a real-world, immersive learning experience that brings culture to life.

8. Acknowledgements

The ENACT project is co-funded by the European Commission, Erasmus Key Action 2 Strategic Partnerships for Higher Education, project number: 2019-1-UK01-KA203-061567. The project is led by Newcastle University (UK), and the consortium partners are: Boğaziçi University (Turkey), Cultura

Foundation (Finland), Universitat Autònoma de Barcelona (Spain), and University of Helsinki (Finland).

References

Dodds, C. B., Satar, M., Kharrufa, A., Seedhouse, P., Sidorova, A., Spazheva, I., Buitrago Peña, J., Dooly, M., Öztekin, E., Akcan, S., Kotilainen, L., & Kurhila, S. (2020). *Identifying requirements for supporting users in creating digital interactive cultural activities for task-based language learning.* https://doi.org/10.13140/RG.2.2.15729.51042

Ellis, R. (2003). *Task-based language learning and teaching.* Oxford University Press.

Latour, B. (1996). *Aramis, or the love of technology.* Harvard University Press.

Seedhouse, P., Heslop, P., & Kharrufa, A. (2020). Cooking as a language learning task. *TESL-EJ, 24*(1), n1.

Smith, B., & González-Lloret. M. (2020). Technology-mediated task-based language teaching: a research agenda. *Language Teaching*, 1-17. https://doi.org/10.1017/S0261444820000233

Thorne, S. L. (2016). Cultures-of-use and morphologies of communicative action. *Language Learning & Technology, 20*(2), 185-191.

Willis, J. (1996). *A framework for task-based learning.* Longman.

9 Building empathy through a comparative study of popular cultures in Caracas, Venezuela, and Albany, United States

José Luis Jiménez[1] and Ilka Kressner[2]

Abstract

During our six-week Collaborative Online International Learning (COIL) module (Oct.-Nov. 2019), 58 students jointly developed task-based projects on expressions of popular culture in Albany (USA) and Caracas (Venezuela). In teams of seven to eight participants, learners from both countries reflected on variations of popular culture through assignments to be resolved in teams that included summaries and critical assessments of readings, contextualization of theoretical concepts, the drafting of a joint video script, and finally creation of a ten-minute video that focused on popular expressions in both cities. All learners were native, fluent, or near-native speakers of Spanish. We experienced the topic of popular culture to be exceptionally well poised to help students engage with each other from the beginning, represent everyday realities and build empathy and transcultural understanding through written reflections and joint creative final projects in the form of documentaries that included slices of life from the two different realities. The small-scale, everyday popular cultural productions allowed for a connection beyond cultural divides, helped students discover novel terrain within their own contexts, and vice versa, find common ground in the new context, thus fostering empathy toward transcultural awareness and equitable collaboration.

---

1. Catholic University Andrés Bello, Caracas, Venezuela; neoselvafoundation@gmail.com; https://orcid.org/0000-0001-6640-0515

2. University at Albany, Albany, New York, SUNY, United States; ikressner@albany.edu; https://orcid.org/0000-0003-0207-1040

How to cite: Jiménez, J. L., & Kressner, I. (2021). Building empathy through a comparative study of popular cultures in Caracas, Venezuela, and Albany, United States. In M. Satar (Ed.), *Virtual exchange: towards digital equity in internationalisation* (pp. 113-127). Research-publishing.net. https://doi.org/10.14705/rpnet.2021.53.1294

Chapter 9

> In their exchange students actively created a shared 'third' culture of collaboration.

Keywords: Venezuela, United States, popular culture, collaborative online international exchange.

1. Introduction

The State University of New York (SUNY) Center for COIL has existed since 2006. Its mission is to "develop collaborative projects that [...] students do together across time zones, language differences and geographical distance using online tools", hence giving the professors and students "the opportunity to engage hands-on with [...] course concepts and new ideas and – most importantly – exploring them from different cultural perspectives"[3]. The authors of this paper met during a COIL academy in March of 2019 for faculty teaching at colleges and universities within the SUNY system and different Venezuelan universities. It was our initial goal to extend the benefits of international and plurilinguistic education beyond our own classes, become part of a network of faculty committed to online international education, and last but not least help our students meet future professional demands such as gaining multicultural skills in the workplace. The classes that collaborated were (1) at Andrés Bello Catholic University through the Department of Journalism and Audiovisual Studies, a course on 'Documentary', and (2) at The University at Albany through the Department of Languages, Literatures, and Cultures, titled 'Popular Culture in Latin America. The joint examination of popular culture and new media were the objectives of both COIL modules.

Our initial research question was the following: is it possible to foster a sense of empathy, transcultural awareness, and equitable collaboration through the joint critical examination of popular culture within a virtual learning environment?

---
3. https://online.suny.edu/introtocoil/

And in relation to this, how can we formulate assignments that help students become aware of their peers' cultural differences in order to transcend stereotypical perceptions?

In a context of multicultural collaboration, students manifest their pursuit of understanding throughout the process of critical reflection and discourse while interacting with their partners abroad. Moving them beyond the restrictions of prior cultural views and developing a sense of awareness, empathy, self-control, and emotional maturity becomes the most important challenge in order to train individuals with a sense of responsibility as global citizens. Empathy then becomes the key ingredient for the success of cross-cultural experiences.

For Santrock (2007), empathy is a positive feeling that acts on the sentiment of others with an emotional response to them. According to Budiningsih (2008), empathy is the understanding of other people's emotions, accepting their point of view, and respecting their differences and their feelings. Moreover, in the Encyclopedia of Social Psychology, Hodges and Myers (2007) state that empathy is the understanding of another person's experience by imagining oneself in that other person's situation: "[o]ne understands the other person's experience as if it were being experienced by the self, but without the self actually experiencing it" (p. 297).

However, cross-cultural communications, oftentimes, confront a variety of obstacles, as Amrina and Indriani point out, due to differences in cultural backgrounds such as customs, traditions, beliefs, ideals, and so on. "If these obstacles cannot be overcome, there will be disagreements or even serious disputes" (Amrina & Indriani, 2020, p. 159). This is when cultural empathy is needed for successful cross-cultural interactions; that way, learners can manage to understand cultures far different from their own, see their own culture from a more critical distance, and their interactions can run well and effectively (Amrina & Indriani, 2020; Jiang & Wang, 2018).

To foster a sense of empathy, transcultural awareness, and equitable collaboration, a joint critical examination of the meaning of popular culture is promoted in our COIL module. During the process, learners obtain new knowledge about popular expressions and traditions; new experiences with their peers abroad; and question and ultimately overturn previously held assumptions. Introducing cultural-empathize states to the cognizant transformation of cultural perspectives in the learning collaboration by a series of multicultural team challenges engages students to intentionally transcend the typecasts and frameworks of local culture, getting rid of the restrictions of their own culture, and placing themselves in another cultural mode to know, realize, and comprehend another culture (Yumin, 2019).

This goal is achieved by creating a 'community of inquiry' as Schertz (2006) states. For the author, a community of inquiry enables students to conjointly explore philosophical concepts, personal anecdotes, and stories through a "discursive structure that allows for and encourages the facilitation of these empathic modes through a dynamic system of interlocking subjectivities" (Schertz, 2006, p. 9). This methodology, as Schertz (2006) indicates, motivates learners to direct their chosen discourses and promote in them an intersubjective form, or 'Gestalt', allowing individuals "to engage each other in effective communication in a discursive context that is also cognitive and metacognitive" (p. 9). By the end of the module, learners manifest a critical reassessment of their psychoemotional responses to the multicultural experience in the form of a final questionnaire; they are able to track the development of their own awareness by comparing it with one of their abroad peers (a group of students involved in our 2019 exchange organized on their own a virtual reunion almost two years after their collaboration), and finally, they are able to identify new multicultural competencies, and acknowledge cognitive challenges from the collaborative experience.

Students' ages at both institutions ranged from 19-71 years, they came from eight different countries in the Americas (North and South), and their educational levels ranged from undergraduate to graduate (Master's and Ph.D.). While the Venezuelan learners were mainly of college-student age, the learners from Albany participated in a shared-resources class for advanced undergraduate students and graduate students alike. Given the fact that UAlbany is one of the most diverse institutions of higher education in the US and an aspiring Hispanic-serving institution, and as a result of its geographical situation in the State of New York, students in the program are either US American students who learned Spanish as a new language, Latino/a/x students of Caribbean and Mexican descent, and Latin American students from the Hispanic Caribbean (Puerto Rico, Cuba, the Dominican Republic), Peru, Ecuador, and Mexico. All students who participated in this study were native or fluent speakers of Spanish, with a minimum of five years of college-level Spanish education.

In the context of an international educational exchange with Venezuela, it should be noticed that for the last ten years, the socio-political situation of the country has worsened to the point of developing into a deep humanitarian crisis. The students that participated in this virtual exchange were media and journalism college students, their ages ranging from 17 to 23 years. We want to highlight that Venezuelan learners experience the pressure of violence, lack of human rights, absence of public services, the lack of a transparent information structure, and a deteriorated educational system on a daily basis. These adverse social conditions affect the learner's overall well-being and by extension, their capacity to fully engage in a virtual exchange experience in the same way that their peers abroad can. In addition, the internet connectivity in Venezuela, according to a recent global average ranking of a total of 139 countries provided by *Speedtest*, was ranked 137, only ahead of Palestine and Afghanistan[4]. Power outages and internet connectivity made synchronous meetings difficult, and provided obstacles to establish communications for group activities. Students had to be resourceful and flexible as to the use of social media and collaborative practices.

2. Methodology

During a six-week period, two classes adopted the COIL methodology[5] and engaged in a shared module titled *Popular Culture and Contemporary Media*.

---

4. https://www.speedtest.net/global-index

5. https://coil.suny.edu/about-suny-coil/

Chapter 9

From October to November 2019, 58 students, 26 from UAlbany (SUNY) and 32 from the Andrés Bello Catholic University of Venezuela jointly developed task-based projects on expressions of popular culture in teams of seven to eight participants. Following a challenging learning curriculum, transformative learning, formulated by Mezirow (1997), goes beyond memorization of information and has both individual and social dimensions and implications. Rennick argues that this pedagogic method emphasizes high impact learning; it is experiential, collaborative, active, and engaging. While applied consciously, students become an active part of world citizenship and are committed to the great purposes of humanity (Rennick, 2015). Learners from both countries explored practices and reflected on variations of popular culture through descriptive and critical assignments and tasks, the drafting of a joint video script, and the creation of a ten-minute video that focused on popular expressions in both cities. Students chose their topics among their teams. Among the choices selected were practices of Indie music, graffiti and other street art, inclusive performance spaces, the creation of community sites among others, and media of contemporary social interaction that particularly communicated popular cultural content.

The methodology of the collaborative virtual module was concentrated on intensive weekly group activities and a learning challenge across the two institutions. The activities were chosen by both professors, they included readings, the watching of videos, and lectures in Spanish and English by cultural and media theorists and practitioners. The readings were between 2,000 and 7,000 words long and were dedicated to the topics of the impact of new media (processes of democratization, hypermediations, ecosystems) and cultural contrasts and comparisons (essays by Roland Barthes, Noam Chomsky, Stuart Hall, and Edward Said)[6].

Teams were tasked to summarize and explain key theoretical terms and were invited to contextualize them using examples of their own life-worlds and cultural experiences.

---

6. https://interactive.aljazeera.com/aje/2017/the-listening-post-media-theorised/index.html

During the process, students read, orally discussed, and commented in writing on three essays chosen by the professors. Later, they carried out the activities on the readings in work teams that met virtually using communication tools of their choice, such as Facebook, FaceTime, Voice Thread, or WhatsApp chats. Our curriculum promoted activities that required students to have an effective communication process in Spanish (US American students as part of their class requirements should communicate in Spanish), the development of common agendas, and the formation of groups with learners of diverse origins to work cooperatively (professors arranged teams in such ways that the groups were as diverse as possible, taking into account age, gender, country of origin, and educational level). In addition, it encouraged learners to propose new, unconventional solutions to institutional, community, and social challenges. Learners skillfully used communication and information technology equipment and applications to interact with others in a global context, despite challenges of internet connectivity.

By discussing with their abroad peers on privacy issues and which safe applications to use to establish interactions and communications, the given assignments motivated them to update their knowledge on digital devices and in the security and protection measures needed to operate these systems. Students received a joint syllabus for the six weeks of the COIL module, each instructor defined the overall weight of the COIL module within students' overall grade (30% and 35% each, roughly proportional to the length of the collaboration during the semesters).

The three main learning objectives defined for this virtual exchange were:

- to practice the use of technologies of communication and information in order to interact with others in a global context;

- to become aware of and interact within a context of multicultural specificities and diversities; and

- to work in a collaborative manner.

The module was designed in four phases: a preparation phase (collaboration basics), engagement phase, reflection phase, and results phase.

2.1. Preparation phase: collaboration fundamentals

Prior to starting the COIL collaboration, students introduced themselves in the joint Facebook virtual classroom (a closed and invisible group) with introductory pictures and brief descriptions of their interests and expectations of the collaboration. After the learners were assigned their teams, during the first week of the module, they engaged in an 'ice-breaker' activity related to the topic of the module: they were tasked with selecting and presenting their personal popular hero to their teammates. In addition, teams also had to define their standards for fruitful collaboration and formulate a total of four criteria in their teams, according to which they evaluated each other's participation at the end of the COIL module. This initial 'ice-breaker' activity, the only required synchronous meeting of the exchange, already opened up the broad scope of notions of the popular and definitions of hero figures, as some students presented for instance fictional comic heroes known to a global audience, others opted for singers or songwriters of regional and national statue, while others chose folkloric figures known only in their regions. Students were not required to summarize this discussion for their professors; instead, they had to take and share a screenshot of their synchronous group meeting and post it on the virtual classroom created on a joint closed Facebook group.

2.2. Engagement phase

During the next three weeks, learners performed joint writing tasks based on the reading of essays and viewing of videos that discussed critical terms, examples of cultural expression, the role of media in shaping popular cultures and stereotypes, and related transfer questions. The assignments consisted in the collaborative writing of short 300 word essays per assignment per team drafted and shared on Google Docs.

2.3. Reflection phase

The third assignment consisted in a progress report where students described the individual pieces of work performed by each of them within their teams, related to the progress of the script of the final joint documentary project. This helped conceive the final project as a true collaborative effort with shared responsibilities.

2.4. Final project

The final COIL project consisted in the creation of, and reflection on, a documentary of a ten-minute video per team dedicated to the theme selected by all team members, in which each teammate participated toward a joint popular culture experience (either personal practices or examinations of popular culture practices of others) in their specific living environments, Albany and Caracas. These videos were shared among all participants at the end of the COIL experience. In the future, we plan to stress the public aspect of this project-based learning and post examples of students' works on online video platforms. Among the topics selected were graffiti and other street art, grassroots music, inclusive performance spaces, and community sites. The final documentaries were shared in the joint closed Facebook group. The format allowed all students (and their instructors) to get insight into daily lives in their own and the respective other city, in addition to being introduced to a selected practice of popular culture. Students organized by teams, wrote the scripts jointly. Then, they went out in their respective cities and with their cellular phones recorded the topics selected by each team. Furthermore, the group members collected the audiovisual material from both countries and selected an editor per team to do the editing of the final production. Other team members from both countries did the voice over and the soundtrack. Each team had to submit one joint video project; teams divided this task differently: most created individual videos (visuals, interviews, etc.) that were then stitched together, while in other teams, one or two team members recorded while others worked in cutting, the adding of the sound track, and features such as split screen, subtitles, etc.

Chapter 9

3. Discussion: building a community of best practice through partnerships and knowledge sharing

New communication technologies facilitate and promote free exchange of knowledge and information, becoming ideal platforms for high impact experiential learning in a virtual exchange experience. Scolari (2008), an academic specializing in transmedia education, indicates that transmedia narrative is characterized by the telling of stories complemented through various media, involving the participation of audiences for the joint construction of the narrative process, which aligned well with the aims of our collaboration. The primary goal of our Popular Culture and Contemporary Media module was to train global citizens and professionals to be able to function in a multicultural world through activities that encourage critical thinking, professional ethics, collaborative work, agency, and flexibility when faced with technological challenges. Using a wide range of technologies of information and communication, students were the protagonists and responsible creators of the content for their own learning. In order to build competencies on empathy and global citizenship, the module focused on three general skills: learn to interact in the global context; learn to collaborate with others; and learn to recognize cultural similarities and differences.

In the preparation phase of the module (icebreaker), learners met their international teammates and skillfully used communication and information technology applications to interact with each other in this inter-American context. As illustrated in the learner quote below, among the group leadership skills to develop during this phase were: collaboration, shared purposes, respect for diversity, assignment of responsibilities, and group learning.

> "Through the length of a couple of months, I got the opportunity to know a small group of wonderful people over 2,000 miles away. Before this, I never even thought about this possibility, but now (thanks to that) I only think of doing it again. Now, I truly believe that this kind of experiences should be more widely available in universities and schools

from all over the world, because it is a necessary experience in the path of receiving an 'education', one which does not limit itself to a piece of paper or giving theoretical knowledge about the functioning of the world, but one that teaches about other people, about being humble and empathic... About being human" (Daniel Strocchia, 2021, student of class on 'Documentary', Venezuela, 2020).

This was echoed by a learner from Albany (who prefers to remain anonymous), who describes their broadening of transcultural experience and communication skills:

> "my transcultural experience was excellent... I am fond of [it] and think that more classes should be taught in this modality, as they give us different perspectives on popular culture in general. [I was able to] expand my communication skills and got to know different dialects" (Student 1, UAlbany, 2021, student of 'Advanced Oral Communication', UAlbany, 2020).

Thus, during the engagement phase of the experience, students learned to collaborate with others by working in high impact experiential learning environments. Through the readings, viewings of videos, and analysis, they recognized the complexities of cultural representation and creation, and the role of the media in shaping popular imagery. This included the pernicious effects of media's power to perpetuate stereotypes. In this hands-on way, learners appreciated and cultivated in a thoughtful, ethical, responsible, and committed manner their relationship with other people in a multicultural environment to contribute to the collective well-being. A second student from UAlbany describes as follows:

> "I didn't expect to create a relationship with students from such a different background... [but] especially the readings helped us get to the same mental ground, and allowed us to get involved more deeply in a discussion of big topics" (Student 2, UAlbany, 2021, student of 'Advanced Oral Communication', UAlbany, 2020).

Chapter 9

In the reflection phase, participants practiced recognizing cultural similarities and differences through the use of cognitive strategies and processes that promote autonomous learning: observation, research, comparison, understanding, analysis, synthesis, discussion, and evaluation. In their teams, learners investigated, discussed, argued, and designed a documentary script on a comparative study of popular manifestations between the two cities.

Providing purpose and agency, students were challenged to develop a ten-minute documentary comparing popular culture of two cities, Albany and Caracas. During this process, we discussed with our teams and classes what it means to act with an ethical sense and to understand their own and their teammates' socio-cultural environments. Participants selected the topic according to their interest and motivations. They identified and assumed as their own the problems of their socio-cultural context. In this exercise, students observed their realities anew and allowed themselves to be challenged by them, and they connected knowledge with their multicultural reality. Among the examples discussed were the notion of the popular – is an activity popular if it is performed by many, if it is free of charge, or can an activity performed by a small group also become popular? Another discussion centered on the presence or absence of the state to define and make space for a cultural activity such as a concert or dance as popular. Students compared the benefits of large cultural organizations offering concerts free of charge to large audiences with grassroots events that bring together artists and listeners in smaller and more improvisational fora. During this process of action-oriented re-framing, the students developed new frames of reference. In her feedback, one student describes how she was able to track the development of her own awareness, identify new competencies, acknowledge cognitive challenges from the experience abroad, and identify competencies that facilitated active responses to the new perspectives developed in the learning process. This is illustrated from the quote below from a student who participated in the collaboration held in 2019.

> "Making a recount, having an experience of collaboration with students from a different area, culture and reality was only the beginning, because

while we lived this exchange, I think that we hardly realized all the tools that we managed to apply as a group, in terms of our audiovisual training. We were completely immersed in the project and this is proven in the richness of the final documentary which, for me, is made up of all that learning" (Sofia Ruiz, 2021, student of class on 'Documentary', Venezuela, 2019).

This project promoted activities that required students to engage in a process of effective communication, the development of common agendas, and the formation of groups with people of diverse cultures to work cooperatively. In addition, it encouraged them to propose new solutions.

The module fomented civic responsibility, self-reflection on values and principles that guided participants, the acquisition of skills to evaluate, self-assess, and gain knowledge of leadership approaches and theories. And finally, the challenge-based learning model encouraged participants to get updated on digital technologies and in the security and protection measures of these systems. In addition, they properly managed, frequently used programs and applications, and interacted in working groups using such technologies. This is exemplified in the quote from a student who participated in our collaboration held in 2020. The student manifests his pursuit of understanding throughout the process of critical reflection and discourse with his collaborators abroad. He demonstrates having obtained new knowledge, having new experiences, and confirms he has overturned previously held assumptions. His explanation displays a critical reassessment of his psycho-emotional responses to the experiences.

> "The COIL experience taught me many things; from a culture that I never thought of, to humbleness and accepting others. Getting to know people with such different values and perspectives of what life actually is, allowed me to realize and accept the immense variety of people and cultures that exist in our world. It also taught me that those differences do not actually separate us, but join us together. It is by accepting each other" (Daniel Strocchia, 2021, student of class on 'Documentary', Venezuela, 2020).

4. Conclusions and outlook

While we write this report, we are currently engaged in our second COIL collaboration of the same topic and course length, now with a new cohort and during times of the COVID-19 pandemic. This time, we are implementing evaluative measures, in addition to qualitative data, to also obtain a set of quantitative data. Among those are initial and final questionnaires for the two student groups that focus specifically on developing empathy and challenging stereotypes related to their own and the other's culture, and individual feedback during the COIL experience.

We experienced the topic of popular culture to be exceptionally well poised to help represent everyday realities and build empathy and transcultural understanding through written reflections, interviews, and joint final projects in the form of documentaries that included 'slices' of life from two different realities. While from a historical perspective, popular cultural production has often (rightfully) been criticized as partaking in imperialist endeavors and highlighted dichotomies – think of Walt Disney's work during the Cold War that offered Latin America as a fantasy land and celebrated the pleasure principle which freed from ethical considerations and responsibility – the small-scale, everyday popular cultural productions discovered in our module highlight instead similarities in variations, help students discover novel terrain within their own contexts, and vice versa, find common ground in the new context. In their high impact experiential learning exchange, they actively created a shared 'third' culture of collaboration. The critical examination of the popular within a virtual learning environment helped foster empathy toward transcultural awareness and equitable collaboration among learners and their instructors.

5. Acknowledgements

The authors wish to thank Annette Richie, Andrea Thomas, and Hope Windle for their contagious passion to engage in new teaching ventures, their inspiration and encouragement was crucial from day one of our collaboration and remains key for us until today. Sincere thanks as well to Müge Satar, Sylvie Thouësny, and the two anonymous reviewers of our paper for their feedback and editorial guidance.

References

Amrina, S.H., & Indriani, L. (2020). Study of EFL students' cultural empathy from cross-cultural communication perspective. *UHAMKA International Conference on ELT and CALL (4th UICELL) 4* (pp. 159-164).

Budiningsih, A. (2008). *Moral learning based on the characteristics of students and their culture*. PT Rineka Cipta.

Hodges, S., & Myers, M. (2007). Empathy. In R. F. Baumeister & K. D. Vohs (Eds), *Encyclopedia of social psychology* (vol. 1, pp. 297-298). SAGE Publications, Inc. https://doi.org/10.4135/9781412956253.n179

Jiang, Y., & Wang, J. (2018). A study of cultural empathy in foreign language teaching from the perspective of cross-cultural communication. *Theory and Practice in Language Studies, 8(*12), 1664-1670. https://doi.org/10.17507/tpls.0812.12

Mezirow, J. (1997). Transformative learning: theory to practice. *New Directions for Adult and Continuing Education, 1997*(74), 5-12. https://doi.org/10.1002/ace.7401

Rennick, J. (2015). Learning that makes a difference: pedagogy and practice for learning abroad. *Teaching and Learning Inquiry: The ISSOTL Journal, 3*(2), 71-88.

Santrock, J. W. (2007). *Child development* (11th ed.). McGraw-Hill.

Schertz, M. (2006). Empathic pedagogy: community of inquiry and the development of empathy. *Analytic Teaching and Philosophical Praxis, 26*(1), 8-14.

Scolari, C. (2008). *Hipermediaciones: elementos para una teoría de la comunicación digital interactiva*. Gedisa.

Yumin, X. (2019). A study on the cultivation of cultural empathy ability of Russian majors in cross-cultural communication. In *Conference Proceeding from ECOMHS* (pp. 144-147). Francis Academic Press. https://webofproceedings.org/proceedings_series/ECOM/ECOMHS%202019/ECOMHS19031.pdf

Section 4.
Staff and student voices

10. Educational innovation in times of crisis: learner voices from the Albany-Caracas COIL exchange

Sofía Ruiz[1], Santiago Hernández[2], Alicia García[3], and Jesús Chacón[4]

Abstract

In the digital era, where everything seems to move at the speed of light, unfortunately certain regions and countries are limited by economic, political, social, or cultural circumstances, as is the case for Venezuela. New technologies are particularly fundamental in the educational field, and every day Venezuelan students need to deal with the second worst Internet in the world (according to a study conducted by Speedtest in 2019), sporadic blackouts, a hyperinflation that makes almost impossible to upgrade equipment, and all the stress and trauma that come along. Despite these challenges, at the Andrés Bello Catholic University (UCAB), ranked number one in the country, a class of communications students were assigned a crucial task: take a joint 100% online Collaborative Online International Learning (COIL) program with students from the State University of New York (SUNY) located in Albany, United States. The final product was a meta-documentary, while the real outcome was an enriching cross-cultural experience. This chapter

---

1. Andrés Bello Catholic University, Caracas, Venezuela; srv177021@gmail.com; https://orcid.org/0000-0001-7340-0070

2. Andrés Bello Catholic University, Caracas, Venezuela; sanhernandezmalave@gmail.com; https://orcid.org/0000-0002-6682-2352

3. Andrés Bello Catholic University, Caracas, Venezuela; aligarciafi98@gmail.com; https://orcid.org/0000-0002-3407-2913

4. Andrés Bello Catholic University, Caracas, Venezuela; alejandrochaconluna@gmail.com; https://orcid.org/0000-0001-7810-0755

How to cite: Ruiz, S., Hernández, S., García, A., & Chacón, J. (2021). Educational innovation in times of crisis: learner voices from the Albany-Caracas COIL exchange. In M. Satar (Ed.), *Virtual exchange: towards digital equity in internationalisation* (pp. 131-138). Research-publishing.net. https://doi.org/10.14705/rpnet.2021.53.1295

complements Jiménez and Kressner's (this volume) chapter, and presents the learner voice from UCAB.

Keywords: virtual exchange, multicultural learning, transmedia, globalization, crisis.

1. Introducing the Albany-Caracas COIL Exchange

Growth, organization, experiment, multicultural, transcendental, commitment, patience, memorable, enriching, diversity, challenge, effort, progress, empathy, innovation, union, fun, engagement, surrender, communication, alliance, cooperation, novelty, enhancing, perseverance, dare, inspiration, unique, compromise, resilience.

These were the words used by the students and the professor from Caracas, Venezuela, to define what the SUNY COIL project experience meant to them. This was our transcultural and transmedia experience created from September 2019 to January 2020, between the documentary course of the Communication Department at UCAB, in Caracas, Venezuela, headed by Professor José Luis Jiménez, and the Latin American Popular Culture course at SUNY, in Albany, USA, directed by Professor Ilka Kressner. The purpose of this exchange was to develop and implement a new form of interaction and learning in the current global context.

For this project, seven groups of seven, and one group of eight students were formed, each involving half of the group members from Caracas, Venezuela, and half from New York, United States. The work dynamics consisted of intensive readings, group activities, meetings, and conversations by video call. Before and after the activities, members of each team met and discussed the task using the diverse tools offered by technology: Facebook chats, emails, Facetime, Zoom, VoiceThread, and WhatsApp. The final work of every team was the production of a ten-minute mini documentary. The theme of the documentary was the popular cultures of each respective city, in this case, Albany and Caracas. Various audiovisual materials were collected: photographs and videos taken with smartphones and professional cameras, images of local artists, recorded interviews, audio, and music, street shots, as well as shots taken in a television studio, on both university campuses, and at houses of some participants. A final 40-minute meta-documentary was produced, containing extracts of each documentary and new material recorded during the course of the semester, which summed up the entire experience. The documentary is entitled: 'Educational Innovation in Times of Crisis'[5] and includes several topics: the economic, social, and political crisis that Venezuela is currently experiencing and the difficulties that this brings, Internet connection limitations, and intermittency in basic services such as electricity, combined with the challenge of establishing a communicative line between students with different realities and cultures.

The project participants faced many challenges such as Internet connectivity and poor broadband in Venezuela, which sometimes resulted in communication failures. Venezuelan students missed some meetings and delays were experienced in sending and receiving messages. There were also language issues. All students from Venezuela and most students from the USA spoke Spanish, yet New York students who did not speak Spanish participated in the activities less, and ceased to offer their collaboration and points of view. Finally, there were some disagreements in relation to cultural and generational differences, personal affairs of the students, varying levels of commitment, and surprisingly, divergent perceptions regarding popular culture, which caused the main creative clashes. Venezuela has a different sense of what art and urban music are and younger people identify more with urban music than with popular music, which caused confusion among students. Yet, the project enabled Venezuelan students to develop and understand new strategies and that multicultural encounters have a long-term impact on us. They faced and overcame the challenges and developed skills to be able to do it again. This is evidenced in the good grades that Venezuelan students managed to obtain as well as the relationships created between students in both groups.

---

5. The IEETDC Versión IVEC documentary is publicly available: https://www.youtube.com/watch?v=RB48fgllnr0

2. Voices of the participants: learner testimonials

In this section, we offer our voices as UCAB learners participating in this project.

2.1. Sofia Ruiz

For this collaborative experience, we joined forces to develop, discuss, and learn about popular culture, identifying our commonalities and differences while working on the assigned readings and theories. We immersed ourselves in social interaction from a multicultural perspective and thus developed communicative skills that allow a connection of learning and intercultural and cross-cultural exchange. We experienced self-expression outside our usual zone or 'comfort zone'. Having an experience of collaboration with students from an area, culture, and reality different from Venezuela, in the midst of an unfavorable context, allowed an even more significant academic and personal growth. We were completely immersed in the project, and this is proven in the richness of the final documentary, which, for me, is a strong reminder that limitations, in every sense, are in our mind.

In my collaborative group, there was a leader from UCAB and another from SUNY in my group, who implicitly laid the foundations for managing tasks and deadlines. Initiative and creativity were always present, so there was never a lack of ideas to nurture each task. This further enriched the exchange because it showed that we were all always willing to listen to each other and we could see the appreciation for the contributions of each member, which for the program was one of the main pillars. Everything in this journey has seemed unattainable at first, however, our tutors have supported us and taught us where to go. They encouraged us to participate in the 2020 International Virtual Exchange Conference, where we presented our documentary. This expanded the range of our vision even more because it allowed us to attend other presentations and hear other experiences.

Within the context of the COVID-19 pandemic, it was interesting to have a virtual exchange experience because it prepared us in some way for what was about to happen and how we would continue to communicate from that moment on.

2.2. Santiago Hernández

I embarked on COIL with mixed emotions. Living in Venezuela is most of the time energy-draining. On top of the usual unstable political and social circumstances, in 2019 there were a series of national power outages. Being a member of the youngest in the country, sometimes called generation of change (a term which I find empowering), everyday pressures were particularly distressing. When I commenced COIL, I was the busiest I had been, finishing the last semesters of my degree, while dealing with several other projects outside the campus. These left me in a state of numbness and isolation. Fortunately, I had already had the opportunity to travel abroad and know different cultures, and a couple of months before stepping on the COIL journey, I had started an online job where I was tutoring people from Asia, literally from the other side of the world. Yet the concept of globalization still felt alien: a continuous transaction at an economic and artistic level, more evident in the audiovisual content, goods, trends, and international news we consume. Little did I know COIL would be a platform to dig even deeper into the universal exploit.

During the trajectory of COIL, the big picture started to look different. For a common purpose, two groups of students from two different countries were starting to seem not so different anymore. There was a complete trade, not only of ideas, but of discrepancies and compliances, while discussing what popular culture is, the themes, and the course of action; and even more importantly, of absences from online meetings, deficiencies in the assignments, and everything related to personal affairs that reminded us that we were humans.

Through COIL, we produced a meta-documentary and exchanged culture and human consciousness. We envisaged a bright future that awaited us. A year later to our exchange, the pandemic would ruthlessly attack the entire planet and successively normalize social distancing, and therefore remote events. This would reaffirm that we live in a digital age, and is in my opinion more alluring. It demonstrated that border is a word, and there are no barriers other than mental ones.

2.3. Alicia García

I was very excited by the idea of this project; however, I did not know if we could carry it out due to different problems we were going through as students in a country like Venezuela. Life in Venezuela is quite complicated; a big part of the population does not have access to basic services such as water, electricity, or food, and the Internet is usually very unstable. Just like Maslow's hierarchy of needs theory says, when basic needs fail, it is difficult to do more demanding activities, and 2019 was a particularly difficult year for Venezuelans, since at the beginning of the year political problems escalated, then on March 7, 2019 the largest massive blackout in the history of Venezuela happened due to a failure in the country's main hydroelectric power plant. The entire country was without electricity for five days, causing serious problems in hospitals, clinics, industries, transportation, and water services, and causing multiple looting nationwide. After that event, power failures became more frequent. In Venezuela, the quality of life of each family varies according to their purchasing power, and a large part of the population does not have the necessary resources to pay the high prices of higher education. I have poor water service that comes from Thursday to Saturday, the rest of the time we must use a tank or store water in containers. Food is more expensive every day, due to the devaluation of the official currency. Power goes out at least once a week for an hour or two. The Internet connection is unstable and slow, so I cannot be online all the time, much of the time I have to use mobile phone data. This is my reality, which is quite privileged compared to most of the Venezuelan population.

Yet, we must continue our university studies and this COIL project was one more challenge. We had to communicate by email, Facebook chat, videoconference by Zoom, and WhatsApp to carry out the evaluated activities. We had to analyze literary texts and make a collaborative mini documentary about the culture and festivities in December that we have in each country.

The COIL experience not only gave me the opportunity to interact with people from other cultures, but by giving us a challenge that we thought was impossible. It brought us closer to the new normal of online classes and digital exchange, it prepared us for the digital era of COVID-19 in 2020, and showed us that exchanges and communication for learning through a digital medium is possible even for countries like Venezuela.

2.4. Jesús Chacón

At the beginning of 2019, the Venezuelan population was left in the dark, facing an energy crisis for several days where darkness became a constant and light an exception. However, the student body had to continue with their academic activities. At the beginning of the seventh semester of social communication, specifically in the audiovisual section, I came across a call to participate in a COIL program. I was very excited to join the project despite what it took to live in a national crisis. Problems with the Internet connection made it difficult to communicate and continue with the project. However, this project, from my point of view, was the ray of hope that I needed at that time.

As students of audiovisual production, we took care of putting together the endless visual pieces to achieve footage that would explain the whole experience in the macro documentary. We were taking big steps in the Venezuelan academic area, holding virtual meetings between Venezuelan and New York students. Since the COVID-19 pandemic, we realized that the method we used to maintain contact with our New York partners for the COIL project formed the virtual academic preparation we needed to study in the new Venezuelan academic system during the pandemic.

3. Conclusions

The whole experience showed us that regardless of the apparently adverse circumstances, internationally shared academic objectives can be achieved, when working with a clear course of action and a range of alternatives. A university from the US and one from Venezuela, working as one group, managed to overcome basic communication barriers and cultural disparities. The main mediums to carry out the project were responsibility, commitment, yearning to learn from other cultures, and resilience. Our professors played a fundamental role in offering guidance that promoted student leadership and proactivity. This experience was proof that the typical and obvious limitations can be managed by the students themselves with proper preparation. We proved that a 100% virtual international collaboration is possible.

References

Jiménez, J. L., & Kressner, I. (2021). Building empathy through a comparative study of popular cultures in Caracas, Venezuela, and Albany, United States. In M. Satar (Ed.), *Virtual exchange: towards digital equity in internationalisation* (pp. 113-127). Research-publishing.net. https://doi.org/10.14705/rpnet.2021.53.1294

Speedtest. (2019). https://www.isemag.com/2019/10/ranking-the-worlds-fastest-and-slowest-internet-speeds/

11. Virtual exchange: from students' expectations to perceived outcomes

Elke Nissen[1], Catherine Felce[2], and Catherine Muller[3]

Abstract

What do students expect before starting a Virtual Exchange (VE) with peers? Are their initial expectations mirrored in the final outcomes they perceive after the VE experience? Or, else, do students acknowledge benefits and acquired skills which they did not expect at first? This study draws on qualitative and quantitative data collected across a variety of VE settings within the Erasmus+ EVOLVE project (16 VEs and 248 students in total). In a mixed-methods approach, it confronts students' expectations and perceived outcomes in order to outline the learning potential of VE, beyond the specific learning objectives set in the different Higher Educational (HE) courses in which a VE was implemented. It brings to light that the overlap between students' expectations and the benefits they see is only partial. The declared outcomes deviate more from the course learning objectives than the initial expectations do, and they are, unsurprisingly, more nuanced and manifold. Expectations of intercultural and language practice and skills development are more often aligned with outcomes voiced by students than is the case for digital and disciplinary skills. What stands out is a great occurrence of transferable skills in the outcomes, including collaborative,

---

1. Université Grenoble Alpes / LIDILEM, Grenoble, France; elke.nissen@univ-grenoble-alpes.fr; https://orcid.org/0000-0001-5308-0727

2. Université Grenoble Alpes / LIDILEM, Grenoble, France; catherine.felce@univ-grenoble-alpes.fr; https://orcid.org/0000-0002-4197-9433

3. Université Grenoble Alpes / LIDILEM, Grenoble, France; catherine.muller@univ-grenoble-alpes.fr; https://orcid.org/0000-0002-0873-4573

How to cite: Nissen, E., Felce, C., & Muller, C. (2021). Virtual exchange: from students' expectations to perceived outcomes. In M. Satar (Ed.), *Virtual exchange: towards digital equity in internationalisation* (pp. 139-155). Research-publishing.net. https://doi.org/10.14705/rpnet.2021.53.1296

relational, and communicative skills that are not always promoted in the course objectives.

Keywords: virtual exchange, learning outcomes, student expectations, course objectives.

1. Background to the research

Since telecollaborative projects and partnerships between geographically distant groups began to penetrate teaching practices almost three decades ago, VE – in its different declinations (O'Dowd, 2018) – has expanded in HE, being implemented in different settings, across a wide range of disciplines and with various pedagogical aims (Helm, 2015; O'Dowd & Lewis, 2016). Research in this field supports the constantly growing set-up of VE in HE courses and contributes to highlighting its impact on the development of students' competences. However, results stem most often from case studies, and if they attest to the diversity and richness of practices, they still have a strong context-specific scope, and cannot inform about generalizable benefits inherent to the VE itself.

The goal of the Erasmus+ EVOLVE project (EVOLVE website[4]; Jager et al., 2019) is to fill this gap by exploring large-scale data in order to identify common trends across a wide range of VEs, and to provide a broader picture of the learning potential of VE. Among the different investigations conducted within the EVOLVE project, the study presented in this paper focuses on the comparison between students' initial expectations at the outset of the VE, and the outcomes and gains stated after completion. The aim is to go beyond the measure of students' satisfaction, and to broaden the results of isolated case studies (e.g. Gimeno, 2018; Marczak, 2016).

---

4. https://evolve-erasmus.eu

2. Methodology for data collection and analysis

2.1. Data collection

The data retrieved within EVOLVE stems from 16 VEs with various settings, which took place between September 2019 and May 2020, involving 24 HE institutions worldwide. The diversity of the VE settings is due to languages used, partners or disciplines involved, duration, and targeted outcomes (for a more detailed VE description, see EVOLVE Project Team, 2020).

For this paper, the measure of objective attainment through a five-point Likert scale constituted the starting point for our analyzes. In order to gain deeper insight into these quantitative results, students' answers to specific open-ended questions in administered pre-and post-surveys (N=248) were analyzed in a comprehensive approach; follow-up interviews (N=19) provided additional information for the qualitative analysis. Figure 1 indicates the specific questions for the collection of data investigated in this paper: two post-survey questions with Likert scales for quantitative data collection, and four open-ended questions at pre- and post-stages (post-survey and interview).

Figure 1. Methods for data collection and specific questions investigated in this paper

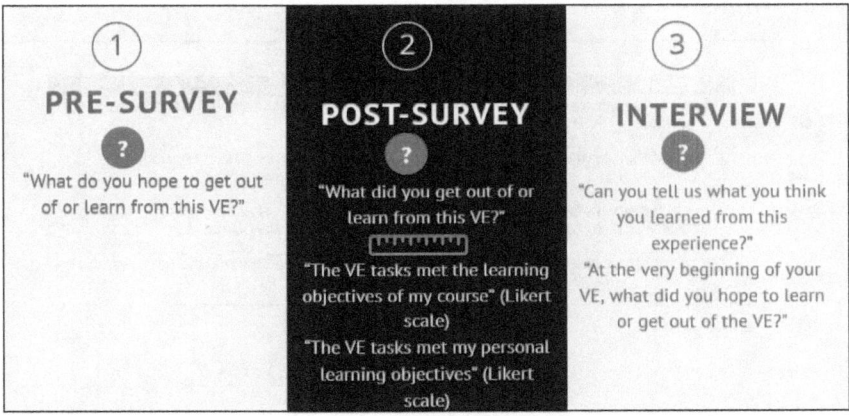

2.2. Processing of the data: establishing coding categories and identifying patterns

This mixed-methods design for the research (Figure 1) allows for elaboration on quantitative results (Brown & Coombe, 2015, p. 81). The data generated from open-ended questions in the surveys and interview were analyzed using the software Nvivo 12 Pro and by adopting an inductive bottom-up approach for identifying and defining coding categories for students' expectations and outcomes (Zhang & Wildemuth, 2009). In order to allow for comparison, the categories established for coding expectations were – as far as possible – aligned with categories for outcomes.

Across the 16 VEs, 12 categories were established for coding expectations as well as outcomes. These include disciplinary, intercultural, language, and digital competences, which are frequently examined VE objectives in the field's literature (O'Dowd & Lewis, 2016) and targeted in HE courses. Along with these, students report on several transferable skills, on the opportunity to make a new experience, or to communicate (in the L2 or more generally), to collaborate with their peers, and to build interpersonal relationships. Adaptability occurred among the reported outcomes as an additional skill that students had not expected.

Figure 2. Identified patterns for comparison between declared expectations and outcomes

	Pattern	Pattern description
✓	1. Initial expectations are fulfilled	Student's indications of VE outcomes match those of their initial expectations
◔	2. Initial expectations are partially met	Several VE outcomes a student indicates match the expectations he/she initially expressed
⊘	3. Initial expectations are totally unmet	None of the VE outcomes a student indicates matches the expectations he/she initially expressed
☆	4. Unforeseen benefits	Students indicate outcomes that they did not mention among their expectations

Patterns based on preliminary pilot study

Through a preliminary study, four main patterns emerged when confronting students' expressed expectations and outcomes.

The first three identified patterns (Figure 2) relate to various degrees of correspondence between students' initially declared expectations from the VE experience, and what they finally state having learned or got out of it. The fourth pattern relates to unexpected outcomes. An additional investigation aimed at determining to what extent students' expectations and outcomes were in line with the objectives set for the different courses the VE was integrated in.

3. Results and discussion

3.1. Perception of learning

Students' level of agreement collected through the Likert scale questions indicate an overall positive to very positive assessment regarding the achievement of learning objectives through the VE, be it the courses' learning objectives or their own (Figure 3 and Figure 4).

Figure 3. Perceived learning outcomes regarding the course objectives (five-point Likert scale)

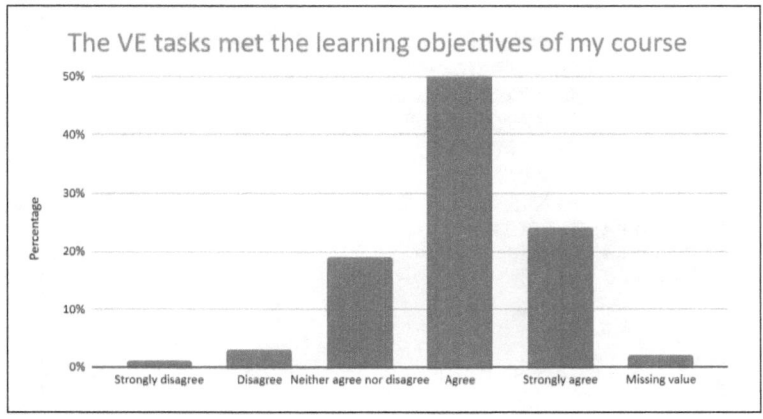

Figure 4. Perceived learning outcomes regarding the personal objectives

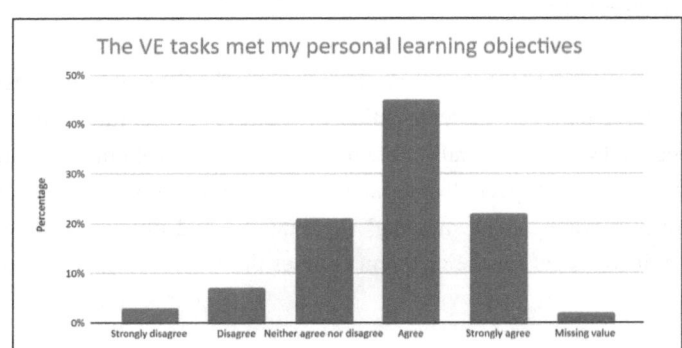

The coding of open-ended questions enabled us to describe more precisely the declared expectations and their alignment with the perceived outcomes – both related or not to the courses' targeted objectives – by assigning categories to students' responses (see 2.2). If the most reported expectation before starting the VE concerns cultural or intercultural aspects, a shift can be observed in the ranking when students report on outcomes once the VE has ended: cultural and intercultural aspects are cited much more frequently, and students value collaborative teamwork as an important skill VE helped develop.

Figure 5. Ranking of mentioned expectations (in percentages)

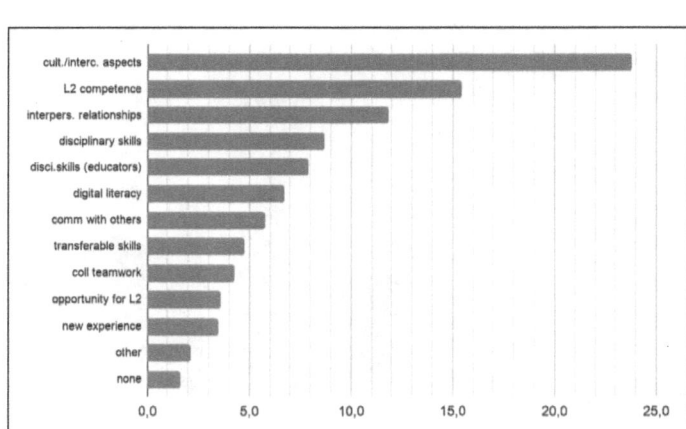

Figure 6. Ranking of declared outcomes (in percentages)

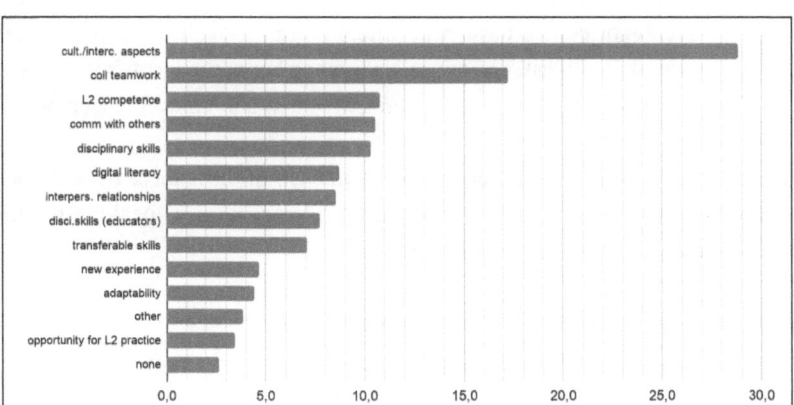

After collaborative teamworking skills, it is communication with others – and not exclusively the development of L2 competence – which also appears as a major outcome. This shows the role the communicative experience plays during the exchanges, not only for the achievement of the VE tasks, but also for establishing interpersonal relationships.

Differences between Figure 5 and Figure 6 indicate that the perceived VE outcomes exceed the initially stated expectations. The students quote many more aspects than they initially expected, and for most of the categories the percentage of mentions is higher.

After comparing expectations mentioned by the students to their declared outcomes, three main tendencies stand out, which refer to three of the pre-identified patterns (see Figure 2):

- all evoked expectations were fulfilled for 29% of the participants, who did not mention having gained other unexpected benefits from their VE participation (Pattern 1);

- for 31 % of the students, no initial expectations were fulfilled (Pattern 3);

Chapter 11

- for 39% of the participants, some of the initially reported expectations appear in the outcomes (Pattern 2). Such an alignment concerns two categories: cultural and intercultural aspects and collaborative teamwork. Both categories are, on the one hand, the most frequently met expectations and on the other hand, the most quoted unforeseen benefits.

The proportion of met and unmet categories in each of these three patterns being globally the same, it is necessary to identify more generally speaking the most frequently met expectations (Figure 7).

Figure 7. Most frequently met expectations (in percentages)

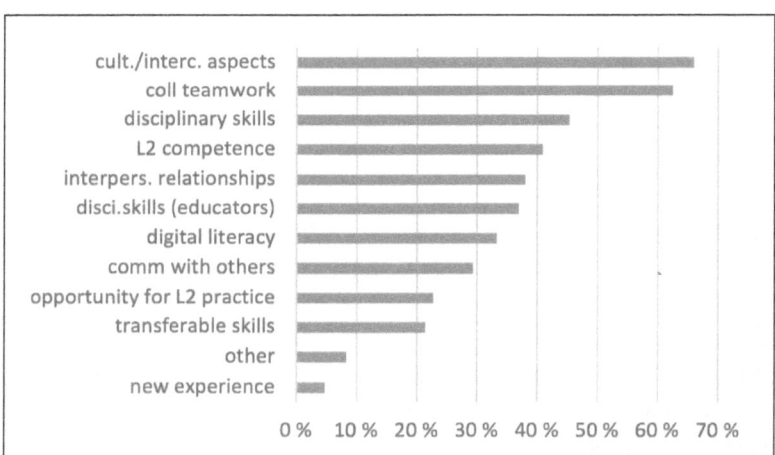

When cultural and intercultural aspects are mentioned in the expectations, in 67% of the cases, they appear in the outcomes as well. The expectation of collaborative teamwork is also satisfied in 63% of the cases. Other expectations are fulfilled in less than 50% of the cases. The results must however be nuanced, as some references which have been coded for specific categories (for instance L2 competence, opportunity for L2 practice, and communication with others) can refer to similar aspects. Slight differences in students' formulations may therefore have led us to attribute their statement of expectation to another category than the expressed outcome.

Figure 8. Unforeseen benefits (number of cases)

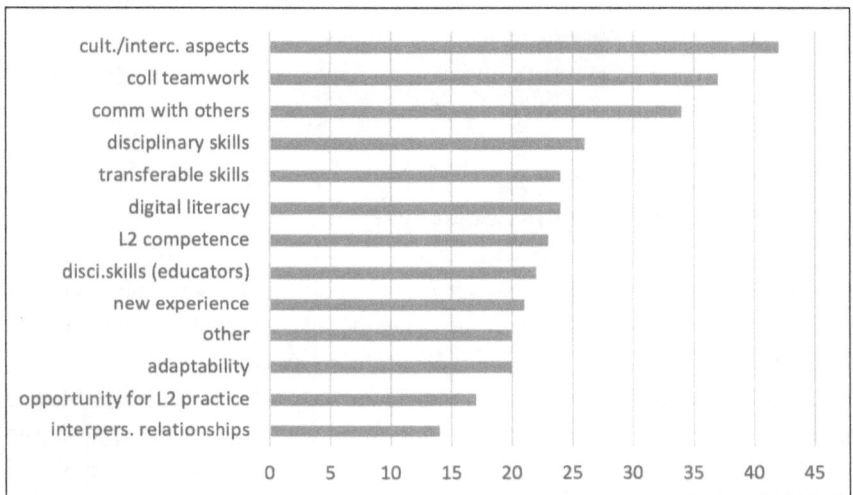

Regarding the fourth pattern – unforeseen outcomes (see Figure 8) – 67% of the students mention gains they did not voice as an expectation before the VE. This highlights the dimension of uncaptured benefits VE might bring to the participants. Interestingly, unexpected outcomes refer again to cultural and intercultural aspects, but concern also collaborative and communicative skills, which are among the most often declared outcomes.

Engagement in VE provides participants with the opportunity to put their knowledge and skills into practice under real conditions of use. Students experienced communication with remote distant partners coming from different geographical areas, which helped them discover other worldviews and reflect on them. They were encouraged to work collaboratively with their peers to achieve the assigned tasks and had to cope with possible issues, developing adaptability, empathy, and social skills. What numerous students particularly valued is the authentic experiential and enjoyable learning provided by the VE, which may have led them to expand their initial expectations. This is illustrated by the following student statement at post-stage.

> "I got to improve my level in french and get better with my compositions in french. I got the chance to meet new people, to work with people at distance. We had to work in groups sometimes which helped us improve our teamwork, to learn what other people think and listen to their opinions. I really enjoyed this experience".

3.2. Perceived outcomes that broaden course objectives

It can be assumed that objectives set for the course and disciplinary contents may influence the expectations of the students. Information gathered from the different partner teachers has enabled us to identify which were the targeted learning objectives for each VE, as well as the learning objectives established in each course. For this part of our study, information about the courses run by the two (or three) partners involved in a VE has been compiled. It appeared that in three VEs, students from one partner institution had not completed the pre- and post-survey, so that data for three courses was missing; in five other courses only one or two students completed both the pre- and post-survey, which was decided not sufficient for considering the course. Consequently, the following data was gathered from 26 (out of 34) courses from 15 different VEs and for which responses of at least three students were available.

The learning objectives indicated by teachers referred to language skills, intercultural competence, disciplinary knowledge (especially teaching skills and critical digital literacy), encompassing either one single type of knowledge or skills or a set of competences. As shown in Figure 9, students' expectations at the outset of the VE are not identical to the learning objectives set for the course but tend to align in a majority of cases (58.4 %). For 23 out of 26 courses, students mention all or more than half of the course objectives as expectations. In contrast, the declared outcomes are less in line with the course objectives (24.1%) and other benefits gained through the VE experience are stated. These results seem to indicate that VE entails a greater potential for developing more or other competences and skills than initially expected or planned, be it by students or by educators.

Figure 9. Congruence rate between course objectives and students' declared expectations and outcomes

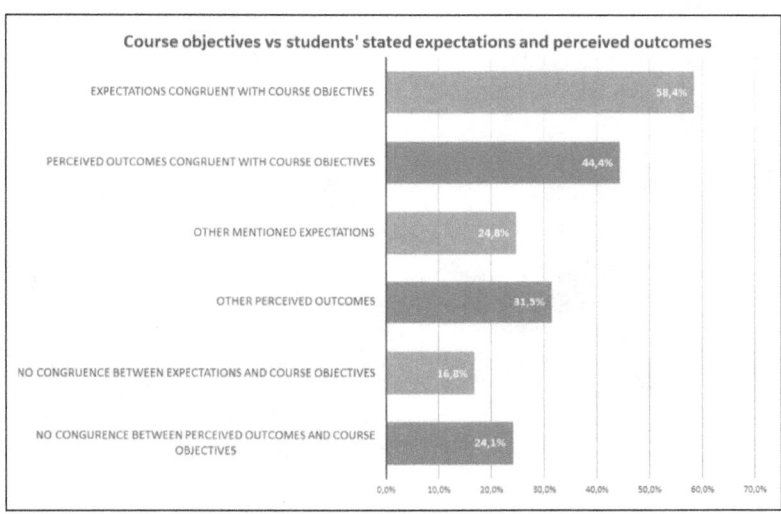

Figure 10. Proportion of students' expectations and perceived outcomes congruent with course objectives (digital literacy)

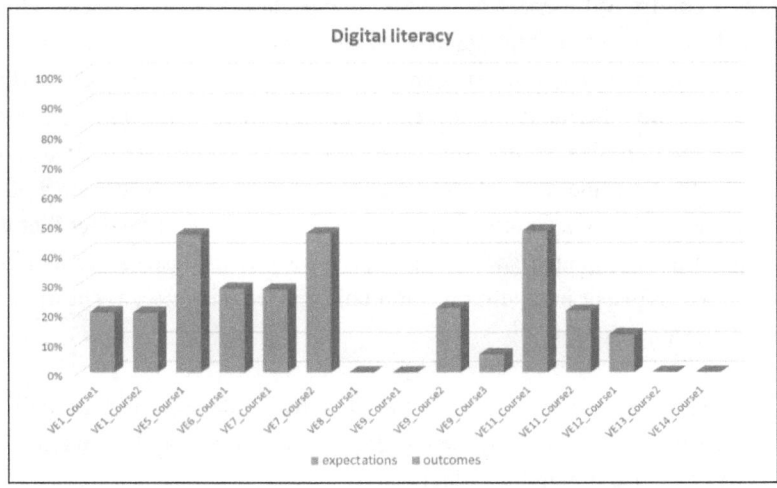

Figure 11. Proportion of students' expectations and perceived outcomes congruent with course objectives (disciplinary skills)

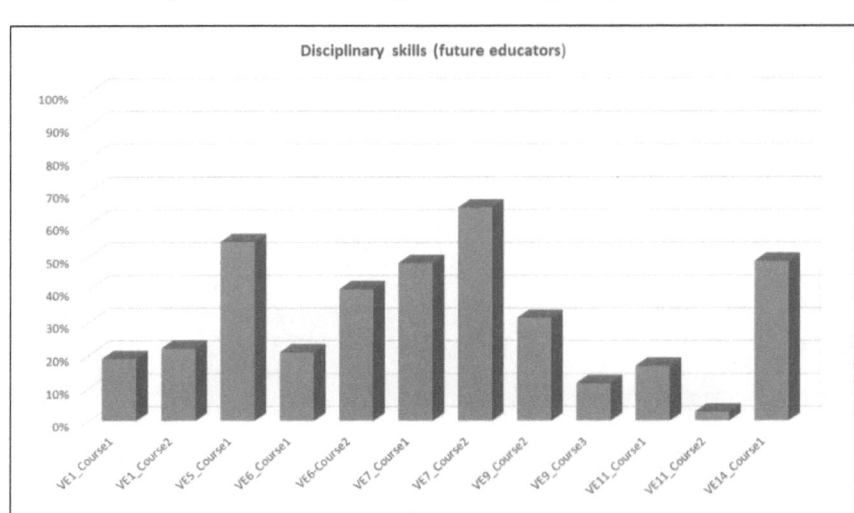

The frequency of coding for the two categories (digital literacy and disciplinary skills related to language teaching and learning) indicated in Figure 10 and Figure 11 confirm differences of overlap in expectations and outcomes. On the one hand, students did not necessarily mention expectations or gains regarding digital literacy and valued other aspects, especially relational or collaborative ones. But on the other hand, improvement in digital skills was among reported outcomes even if this competence was not explicitly targeted as a course objective. In the same vein, if disciplinary skills are not always stressed by the students as the major outcome of their VE, this is due to the fact that they highlighted having gained additional (transversal) skills, such as adaptability, collaborative skills, or intercultural communicative competence, as shown in the following examples.

> "The most valuable thing of [VEs] is that students would not only get profit towards their academic development but mainly towards their personal and individual development".

"I learned about the different communication styles of people, how to collaborate with others who have different communication styles, and how to better respond to others when dealing with conflict".

Figure 12. Proportion of students' expectations and perceived outcomes congruent with course objectives (language skills)

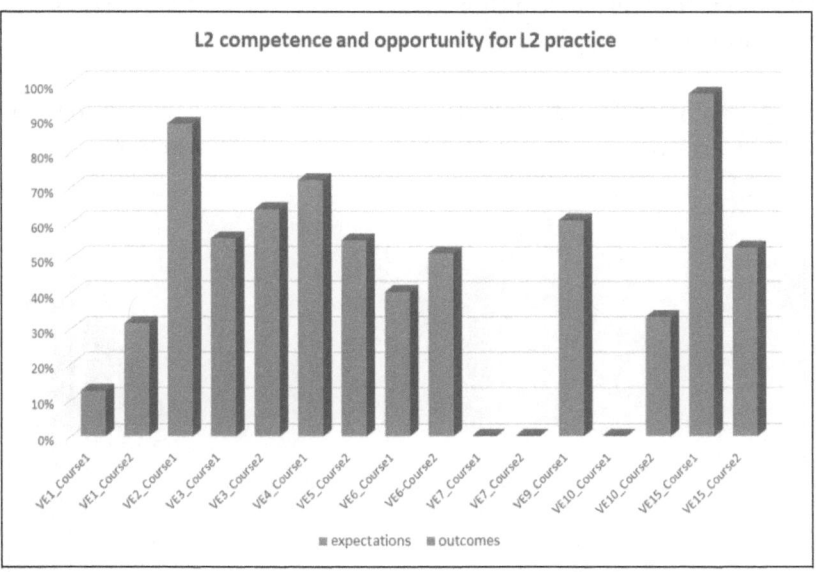

However, a greater alignment can be observed when language and intercultural skills are at play, as VE was in some cases integrated in a language course. Regarding language skills – referring to both categories "L2 competence" and "opportunity of L2 practice" (Figure 12), the high proficiency level of some students may explain why language improvement is not always perceived neither as an expectation nor as an outcome. Consequently, those students considered other targeted outcomes more important or unforeseen benefits much more salient, such as the building of interpersonal relationships, or adaptability. The development of intercultural competence was a learning objective in several courses (Figure 13); only few students in these courses voiced other expectations and if so, they still acknowledged an intercultural benefit among the outcomes of the VE. The results for these two categories are in line with previous studies, which have demonstrated the impact of VE on the development of language skills and intercultural competence (e.g. Helm & van der Velden, 2020; The EVALUATE group, 2019). Nevertheless, the qualitative analysis of the open-ended questions reveals that students' expectations regarding their learning are often very general or narrow, whereas their description of the perceived outcomes is often much broader and goes beyond the mere objectives of their university course.

Figure 13. Proportion of students' expectations and perceived outcomes congruent with course objectives (intercultural aspects)

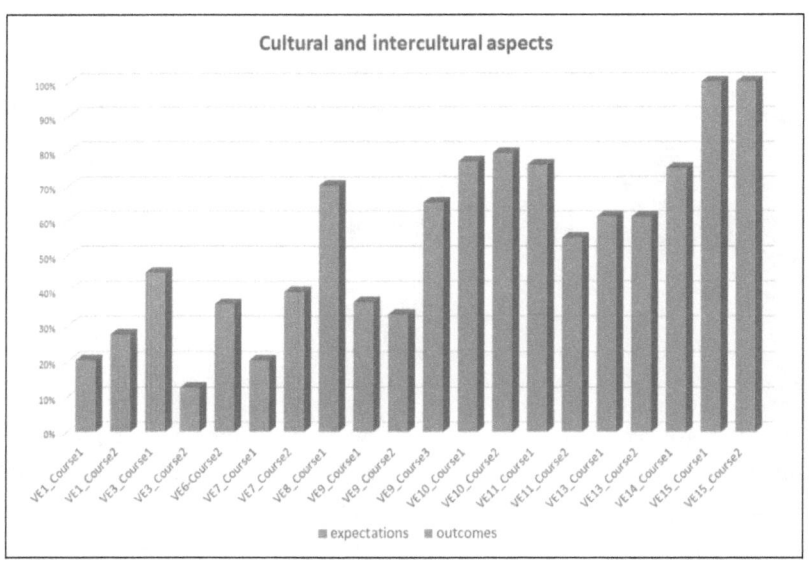

VE offers a unique educational context in which participants are likely not only to enhance but also to challenge their communicative, collaborative, and intercultural skills. In that sense, students may develop transversal skills in addition to the disciplinary contents or the learning objectives set in their HE course and beyond their own learning expectations as well. Nature and depth of personal or academic learning objectives can be modified as a consequence of the VE experience and students' engagement in VE may therefore contribute to the development of more complex and intertwined competences, as illustrated in the following student post-survey statement.

> "I got an opportunity to use English in a more authentic way by cooperating with people from other countries who also use English as a lingua franca. I learned how difficult it is to include seven people in a project and make everyones voices heard. I learned more about how I function in a group work and how I perceive my country and my culture as well as other countries and cultures" (Nissen, Felce, & Muller, 2020, p. 46).

4. Conclusion

This study brings to light occurring shifts and changes between what students expect to get out of or learn from international task-based peer-to-peer interaction in a VE and what they finally declare as major VE outcomes. The greatest match between expectations and outcomes relates to intercultural or cultural aspects. Qualitative insights through open-ended questions nevertheless show that the benefits provided by the VE experience are manifold, and are necessarily largely narrowed down by exclusively quantitative measures of matching categories between initial expectations and final outcomes.

Our study evidences that students' expectations are partly influenced by the objectives targeted in the different courses. Yet, the perceived outcomes also reveal gains in transferable skills (such as collaborative, relational and communicative skills) that are not always promoted in the course objectives. VE results in unexpected benefits, as it is very often a new experience for students, and very different from other pedagogical settings they are used to.

Knowledge of students' expectations and of unforeseen outcomes can be considered as crucial for educators and course designers in order to take better advantage of the learning potential of VE when defining the learning objectives.

Chapter 11

In parallel, targeted learning objectives that embrace this potential are likely to help students to develop more fine-tuned skills.

References

Brown, J. D., & Coombe, C. (2015). *The Cambridge guide to research in language teaching and learning intrinsic eBook*. Cambridge University Press.

EVOLVE Project Team. (2020). *The impact of virtual exchange on student learning in higher education*. EVOLVE Project publication. http://hdl.handle.net/11370/d69d9923-8a9c-4b37-91c6-326ebbd14f17

Gimeno, A. (2018). Learner expectations and satisfaction in a US-Spain intercultural telecollaboration project. *Bellaterra Journal of Teaching & Learning Language & Literature, 11*(3), 5-38. https://doi.org/10.5565/rev/jtl3.776

Helm, F. (2015). The practices and challenges of telecollaboration in higher education in Europe. *Language Learning & Technology, 19*(2), 197-217.

Helm, F., & van der Velden, B. (2020). *Erasmus+ Virtual Exchange. Impact Report 2019*. Publications Office of the European Union.

Jager, S., Nissen, E., Helm, F., Baroni, A., & Rousset, I. (2019). *Virtual exchange as innovative practice across Europe: awareness and use in higher education: EVOLVE project baseline study. Education.* https://research.rug.nl/nl/publications/virtual-exchange-as-innovative-practice-across-europe-awareness-a

Marczak, M. (2016). Students' perspective on Web 2.0-enhanced telecollaboration as added value in translator education. In S. Jager, M. Kurek & B. O'Rourke (Eds), *New directions in telecollaborative research and practice: selected papers from the second conference on telecollaboration in higher education* (p. 245-252). Research-publishing.net. https://doi.org/10.14705/rpnet.2016.telecollab2016.514

Nissen, E., Felce, C., & Muller, C. (2020). Students' general perceptions. In EVOLVE Project Team, *The impact of virtual exchange on student learning in higher education* (pp. 32-49). EVOLVE Project publication. http://hdl.handle.net/11370/d69d9923-8a9c-4b37-91c6-326ebbd14f17

O'Dowd, R. (2018). From telecollaboration to virtual exchange: state-of-the-art- and the role of UNICollaboration in moving forward. *Journal of Virtual Exchange, 1*, 1-23. https://doi.org/10.14705/rpnet.2018.jve.1

O'Dowd, R., & Lewis, T. (2016). *Online intercultural exchange: policy, pedagogy, practice*. Routledge.

The EVALUATE Group. (2019). *Evaluating the impact of virtual exchange on initial teacher education: a European policy experiment*. Research-publishing.net. https://doi.org/10.14705/rpnet.2019.29.9782490057337

Zhang, Y., & Wildemuth, B. M. (2009). Qualitative analysis of content. In B. M. Wildemuth (Ed.), *Applications of social research methods to questions in information and library science* (pp. 308-319). Libraries Unlimited.

12 Continuous professional development on virtual exchange in Europe: insights from the Erasmus+ VE introductory online course

Ana Beaven[1] and Gillian Davies[2]

Abstract

This presentation focuses on the Erasmus+ online introductory training course, which aims to introduce university educators and administrative/technical staff to Virtual Exchange (VE). The training, which requires no previous experience with VE, engages the participants in tasks that help them understand the requirements to successfully integrate an Erasmus+ VE project into existing courses and curricula, while gaining experience in digital literacy, including communicating and collaborating online. After a brief presentation of the structure of the four-week course, we will show how the design of the course – based on an experiential learning approach – elicited reflections and discussions on pedagogical and technological issues crucial to successful VE projects. Finally, we will show how forum interactions between teaching and administrative staff helped all the participants understand the pedagogical, technological, and administrative implications of setting up VE projects, and identify the necessary steps to engage the different stakeholders (teachers, administrative and technical staff, top management, and students) within their institutions. The overall evaluation of all training courses was highly positive: respondents reported discovering that the course boosted their confidence in communicating or working in a culturally diverse setting. They also felt that the training helped

---

1. University of Bologna, Bologna, Italy; ana.beaven@unibo.it; https://orcid.org/0000-0003-3289-3010

2. University of Padua, Padua, Italy; gillian.davies@unipd.it; https://orcid.org/0000-0001-7748-1349

How to cite: Beaven, A., & Davies, G. (2021). Continuous professional development on virtual exchange in Europe: insights from the Erasmus+ VE introductory online course. In M. Satar (Ed.), *Virtual exchange: towards digital equity in internationalisation* (pp. 157-167). Research-publishing.net. https://doi.org/10.14705/rpnet.2021.53.1297

Chapter 12

them develop their intercultural awareness, digital competences, active listening, communication skills, and acquire ideas for new teaching practices.

Keywords: Erasmus+ VE, continuous professional development, internationalisation at home.

1. The Erasmus+ VE initiative

Erasmus, the European Commission's flagship mobility programme, was initiated in 1987, and since then has allowed over 10 million citizens to spend a period of time studying or working abroad (European Commission, 2019). Erasmus + VE is an innovative pilot project established by the European Commission in order to expand the reach of the Erasmus+ programme through VE, seen as a complement to physical exchange programmes. Launched in 2018, its overall aim is to allow as many young people as possible to benefit from a meaningful intercultural learning experience online, as part of their formal or informal education.

The project's objectives are twofold: on the one hand, it is about fostering mutual understanding and dialogue; on the other, it aims to increase digital equity in internationalisation by promoting the development of skills including critical thinking, intercultural communication, empathy, and media and digital literacy (for an overview of the programme, see Helm, Guth, Shuminov, & Van der Velden, 2020).

The project is being implemented by a consortium of eight organisations: Search for Common Ground, Anna Lindh Foundation, UNIMED, Sharing Perspectives Foundation, Soliya, Kiron Open Higher Education, Migration Matters, and UNICollaboration. UNICollaboration is a cross-disciplinary professional organisation for telecollaboration and VE in Higher Education, and is responsible for the training courses offered regularly within the Erasmus+ VE initiative.

These include a four-week introductory training course for Higher Education Institution (HEI) teaching, administrative and technical staff, a six-week advanced training for teaching staff focusing on designing and implementing VE projects, and training for youth workers. The aim of this paper, which focuses on the first of the three training courses, is to examine the motivations of trainees when enrolling in the course, to explain the pedagogical principles in the design of the course, and to review the feedback given by the participants at the end of the training.

2. The introduction to VE training course

The aims of the introductory course (Basic Training) are to first introduce university educators and staff to the concept of VE and its different opportunities; second, to enable participants to understand how to successfully integrate an Erasmus+ VE project into existing courses and curricula in their particular contexts; third, to enable participants to gain experience in digital literacy, including communicating and collaborating online; and finally, to discuss the challenges involved in VE and the solutions to these challenges.

The course is structured so that each week focuses on a different theme, including VE, online presence, and digital literacies (Week 1), VE from the perspectives of students and educators from various disciplines (Week 2), matching pedagogy and technology, and engaging stakeholders (Week 3), and pre-empting potential challenges (Week 4).

During the past three years, a number of changes were made to the contents of the course, based on the feedback received from the participants after each iteration. Thus, tasks were added that clarified the concepts of digital literacies and online presence, and activities were added aimed specifically at increased participation by administrative staff, in particular from international relations offices. At the request of some participants, who wished to stay in touch after the course, we also created a community space where, for example, webinars were organised with experienced VE implementers to showcase their experience and advice. These webinars were also recorded and used as a resource during the training courses.

3. Motivation to enrol in the course

The motives for enrolling in the Basic Training course vary, and recall observations made in the literature: many trainees see VE as a tool which can support their involvement in other European projects (for example physical and virtual mobility programmes), or within the new University Alliances. The training also fills a perceived gap in professional development for both academic and non-academic university staff (Brighton, 2020), in supporting internationalisation at home (O'Dowd, 2017) and online international collaborations (Hildeblando Júnior & Finardi, 2018). More recently, many participants state their need to find alternatives to physical mobilities as a result of the Covid-19 pandemic (Hildeblando Júnior & Finardi, 2020; Kelly, 2021).

> "[My university] is a partner in ERASMUS+ KA2 project. **VE is foreseen as a big part of total project mobilities**. We deeply need knowledge about what it is, where to start and how to implement VE between project partners" (participant, Latvia).

> "Our institution would like to enhance its **activities in internationalisation**. Although we are active in the mobility of students and lecturers, this programme seems to provide a wide range of opportunities. Furthermore, we hope it will encourage students – and of course lecturers – for mobility since it could be **a first step towards an international experience**" (participant, Turkey).

> "This academic year we are focusing on **internationalisation @home**. As part of **lecturer professionalisation** we would like to create an offer for lecturers that are interested to introduce VE in their courses" (participant, Belgium).

"We are trying to develop VEs for our institution and train our academics and support services as part of our **internationalisation strategy** 2019-2025" (participant, UK).

"I believe that VE will be useful for the development of the activities of our **European University Alliance**, therefore I would like to learn more about how it works in order to help the alliance implement it" (Participant, Italy).

"I am the institutional coordinator of one of the **European University Alliances**. VE will be something that we will launch in the alliance, and all the support and knowledge in that field will be needed. We have allocated resources to create new online courses, and now **we need more training in how to put things in practice**" (Participant, Germany).

4. Learning by doing, reflecting, and discussing

Reflections and discussions on all aspects of project design and implementation are crucial to successful VE projects (Guasch, Alvarez, & Espasa, 2010; Vinagre, 2016). For this reason, emphasis was placed on providing opportunities in the form of weekly discussion forums for interaction between teaching and administrative staff, as this helped all the participants understand the pedagogical, technological, and administrative implications of setting up VE projects, and identify the necessary steps to engage the different stakeholders (teachers, administrative and technical staff, top management, and students) within their institutions.

"This overall situation is very hard, and of course will affect mobilities next year all around the world! This is why we need new forms of mobilities like the VE projects, which I see as a complementary and not a substitution of face-to-face mobilities" (administrative staff, Italy).

"I agree with your stance on VE not replacing physical contact. However, it could be an excellent opportunity to introduce our students to other people (and for students to develop mutually beneficial learning experiences). Their time together in a VE project could possibly trigger a need for traveling abroad and to meet face to face" (teacher, Israel).

"What I have seen happen here in Madrid as in the rest of the world has called me to a need for meaning, even in my work. And this is already a victory. The work done and what we are doing on VE can be an instrument of change, of growth" (teacher, Spain).

"Covid, mixed with Brexit for us, has changed the way we look at internationalisation and I personally think online work and virtual activity is a great enhancement/addition to what we already do. VE is not a replacement for real exchanges **but it is definitely more inclusive** and **has impact on more students/staff**" (administrative staff, UK).

"I completely agree with you on **the importance of the democratic nature of VE**. This kind of activities **could help economically disadvantaged students or disabled students** who have difficulties in travelling to experience internationalisation at home" (teacher, Italy).

5. Feedback from participants

Following each iteration, participants were sent a feedback questionnaire, used by the trainers to reflect on the course and make any necessary adjustments.

Below, we report the feedback from two iterations: January 2020, before universities were forced into lockdown due to the Covid-19 health emergency, and June 2020. The January course had a total of 76 participants, evenly distributed between teaching and administrative staff, whereas in June 2020 the number of participants doubled, with 142 enrolled staff, of which about two thirds were administrative staff mostly from international relations offices, in charge of finding alternatives to their physical mobility programmes thwarted by the travel restrictions put in place during spring 2020.

Figure 1 shows the skills that the participants considered they had developed during the course: in both iterations, these were digital competences, active listening skills, and intercultural awareness. Figure 2 shows the extent to which the participants developed their understanding of VE, and were considering future engagement with VE activities.

Figure 1. Course evaluation – skills developed

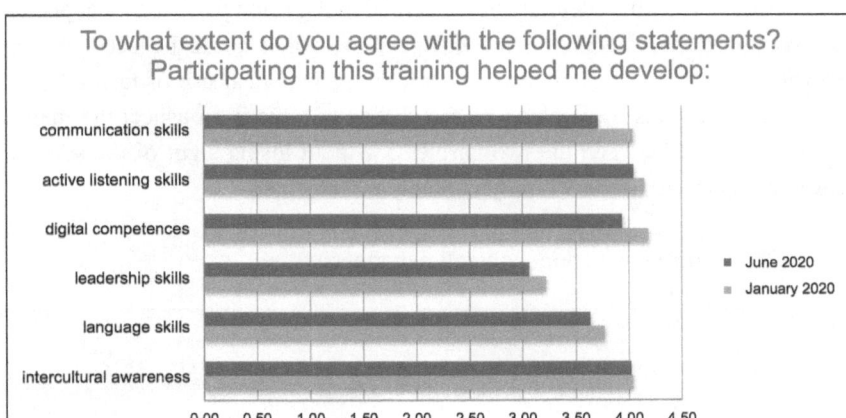

Figure 2. Course evaluation – understanding of VE

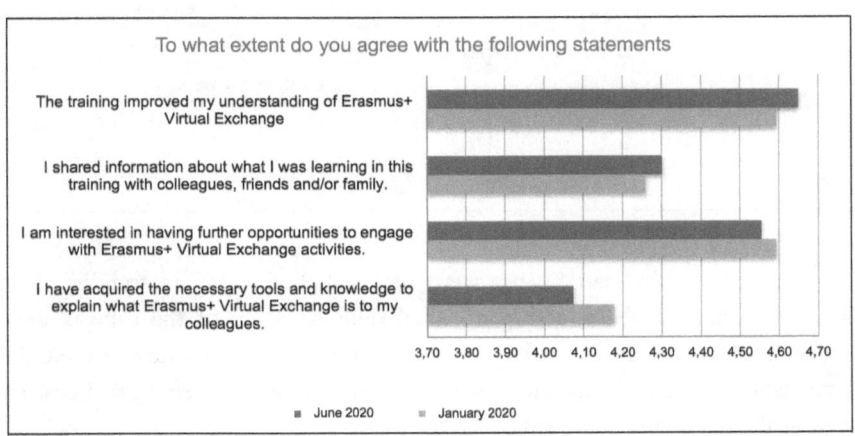

Figure 3 shows the overall course evaluation, which shows general satisfaction with all aspects of the course. The Moodle platform was not appreciated by all, but the use of Zoom during the weekly synchronous sessions (in particular the interactions in small groups through use of the Breakout rooms), was particularly appreciated by many and provided ideas on how this synchronous communication tool could be used in their own VE projects.

Another aspect worth reflecting on concerned tools: some participants expected to have more information on the different tools that could be used in VE. However, the focus of the course was on the pedagogical use of technologies rather than the tools themselves, as the choice of tools is an aspect that needs to be negotiated between the two partners, without losing sight of the specific learning objectives of the VE project being implemented.

Figure 3. Course evaluation – overall experience

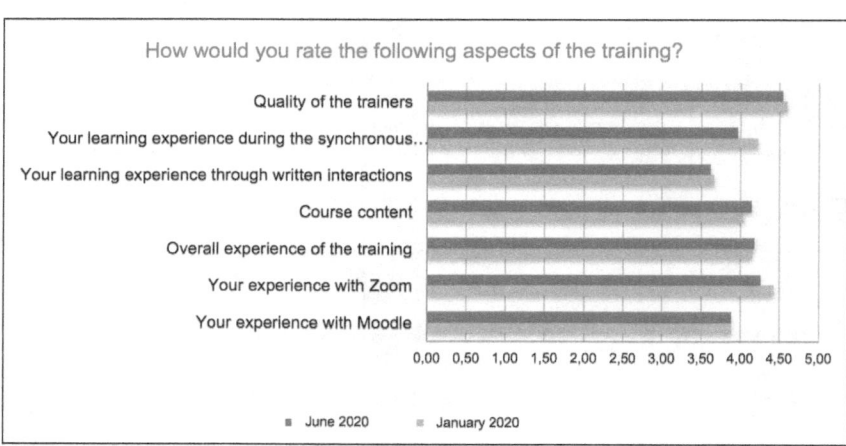

Generally, then, the participants were very satisfied with the training they received. Their feedback comments shed light on some of the aspects they appreciated more, in particular the opportunity to explore how VE could contribute to internationalisation at home and to more inclusive practices, as well as the pragmatic approach of the course.

"Although VE will not, and should not, substitute physical mobility and exchanges, **VEs present us with the opportunity to multiply our internationalisation activities**, and to **promote our institutions and programmes to a broader audience**" (Participant, Italy).

"I enjoyed the synchronous sessions on Saturday mornings. **I liked that the group was mixed**, with administrative staff (of different levels), and teaching staff" (Participant, Italy).

"**I feel that the project integrated perfectly both realities, teaching and admin staff, and provides them with a space, not only to learn the basics of VE but also to dialogue and understand each other's perspectives.** I also appreciated the project's pragmatism" (Participant, Spain).

"By taking part in this programme I was powerfully **reminded how it felt to be the student**. I will bring this renewed insight back to teaching and preparation. **The interactive activities within the synchronous elements stand out for me and remind me that these things can be done well in a virtual world and therefore open a range of possibilities for students who may not have the option to travel**" (Participant, Ireland).

"Having started this course with a very low level of knowledge about the subject area, **I now feel that I am well equipped with ideas, suggestions, and practical steps that I can take to put VE onto the radar of key stakeholders at my university**" (Participant, UK).

6. Conclusion

As the Erasmus+ VE initiative comes to a close in December 2020, we can confidently say that the training provided has focused on some of the areas that the Erasmus+ programme seeks to address with staff mobility, including the promotion of innovative teaching methods, in particular teaching making use of information and communications technology and learning in multidisciplinary groups.

In addition, it has provided opportunities for teaching and administrative staff to discuss these projects together and see VE design and implementation from both sides. Erasmus+ VE has also directly addressed some of the competences that Erasmus+ staff mobility targets: transversal skills, intercultural and social competences, as well as digital competences, with many participants valuing the course as professional development.

There is thus a strong alignment between Erasmus+ mobility and Erasmus+ VE for staff as well as students. The initiative has been a way of making Erasmus+ more inclusive in that it can offer a quality international and intercultural learning experience to HEI staff that are hindered from accessing mobility for personal reasons and work responsibilities. At the same time, it can create opportunities and networks for staff that want to use Erasmus+ mobility as it supports the creation of international networks. We therefore hope that there will continue to be political and financial support for VE in the new European programme starting in 2021.

7. Acknowledgements

Erasmus+ VE was a European initiative (2018-2020) established under a contract with the EU's Education, Audiovisual, and Culture Executive Agency.

References

Brighton, C. (2020). Training for virtual exchange. *Journal of Virtual Exchange, 3 (SI-IVEC2019)*, 69-79. https://doi.org/10.21827/jve.3.35810

European Commission. (2019). *Nine things you didn't know about Erasmus!* https://europeancommission.medium.com/10-things-you-didnt-know-about-erasmus-41bb2c8ebd9c

Guasch, T., Alvarez, I., & Espasa, A. (2010). University teacher competencies in a virtual teaching/learning environment: analysis of a teacher training experience. *Teaching and Teacher Education, 26*(2), 199-206. https://doi.org/10.1016/j.tate.2009.02.018

Helm, F., Guth, S., Shuminov, E., & Van der Velden, B. (2020). Erasmus+ Virtual Exchange. *Internationalisation of Higher Education, 1*, 91-109.

Hildeblando Júnior, C., & Finardi, K. (2018). Internationalisation and virtual collaboration: insights from COIL experiences. *Ensino Em Foco, 1*(2), 19-33.

Hildeblando Júnior, C. A., & Finardi, K. R. (2020). Telecolaboração e internacionalização do ensino superior: reflexões a partir da pandemia covid-19. *Revista Intercâmbio, 5*(45), 254-278.

Kelly, D. (2021). The impact of Covid-19 on internationalisation and student mobility: an opportunity for innovation and inclusion? In S. Bergan, T. Gallagher, I. Harkavy, R. Munck & H. van't Land (Eds), *Higher education's response to the Covid-19 pandemic: building a more sustainable and democratic future*. Council of Europe Higher Education Series No. 25. https://rm.coe.int/prems-006821-eng-2508-higher-education-series-no-25/1680a19fe2#page=227

O'Dowd, R. (2017). Virtual exchange and internationalising the classroom. *Training Language and Culture, 1*(4), 8-24. https://doi.org/10.29366/2017tlc.1.4.1

Vinagre, M. (2016). Developing teachers' telecollaborative competences in online experiential learning. *System, 64*, 34-45. https://doi.org/10.1016/j.system.2016.12.002

Author index

B
Beaven, Ana v, 10, 157
Brautlacht, Regina v, 7, 41

C
Chacón, Jesús v, 9, 131
Cheikhrouhou, Nadia vi, 7, 51

D
Davies, Gillian vi, 10, 157
DeWinter, Alun vi, 7, 29
Dodds, Colin B. vi, 9, 101

E
Emans, Denielle J. vi, 8, 85

F
Felce, Catherine vi, 10, 139
Feng, Ruiling vii, 8, 63
Fondo, Marta vii, 8, 73
Fonseca, Paula vii, 7, 41

G
García, Alicia vii, 9, 131

H
Hernández, Santiago vii, 9, 131
Hulme, Wendi viii, 7, 41

J
Jiménez, José Luis viii, 9, 113
Julian, Kristi viii, 7, 41

K
Kharrufa, Ahmed viii, 9, 101
Klamer, Reinout ix, 7, 29
Kressner, Ilka ix, 9, 113

L
Ludwig, Kenneth ix, 7, 51

M
Martins, Maria De Lurdes ix, 7, 41
Muller, Catherine x, 10, 139
Murdoch-Kitt, Kelly M. x, 8, 85

N
Nissen, Elke x, 10, 139

R
Roche, Catherine x, 6, 17
Ruiz, Sofía x, 9, 131

S
Satar, Müge v, x, 1, 9, 101
Shirvani, Sheida xi, 8, 63
Szobonya, Patricia xi, 6, 17

W
Whelan, Alison xi, 9, 101

www.ingramcontent.com/pod-product-compliance
Lightning Source LLC
Chambersburg PA
CBHW022011160426
43197CB00007B/379